The Science of Powerful Focus:

23 Methods for More Productivity, More Discipline, Less Procrastination, and Less Stress

By Peter Hollins,
Author and Researcher at
petehollins.com

Table of Contents

The Science of Powerful Focus: 23 Methods for More Productivity, More Discipline, Less Procrastination, and Less Stress 3
Table of Contents 5
Introduction 7
Chapter 1. Discipline and Willpower 13
Chapter 2. Goals 29
Chapter 3. Procrastination 45
Chapter 4. Energy 59
Chapter 5. Stress 77
Chapter 6. Singletasking 93
Chapter 7. Productivity 115
Chapter 8. Tactics 133
Chapter 9. Odds and Ends 159
Chapter 10. Conditioning 175
Chapter 11. Nature 189
Conclusion 205
Summary Guide 207

Introduction

When I was in university, I eventually gained quite a reputation. Unfortunately, it wasn't the type of reputation I could impress the opposite sex with, or even be proud of.

My reputation was that of the person who procrastinated until the last moment before assignments were due and got them done at any cost. And this is in a literal sense: I would hand in assignments at 8:59 p.m. if they were due at 9:00 p.m. on a given day. I wouldn't sleep for the 48 hours prior to the deadline and managed to pull off ridiculous feats of focus time after time.

Only once did I fail to meet the deadline. It was a paper about the spread of Confucianism in Asia, and for whatever reason, I simply could not muster the willpower to dive into Chinese proverbs that all required philosophical analysis. To solve the problem, I had a friend corrupt my Word document and I sent the file, which would never work for my professor. This bought me another night of frantic work, and I didn't sleep a wink.

By my senior year, this was a habit I had largely grown out of. It simply wasn't a sustainable way of getting through college, especially as assignments grew longer and harder and were held to higher standards.

I had to find better ways to actually focus, and it dawned on me that I had never really learned study skills. Instead, I had depended on my all-nighters. I felt intense feelings of dread as I was assigned a 50-page term paper on the philosophical teachings of Karl Marx. This wasn't something I could hammer out in under a week.

The same friend who intentionally sabotaged the Word document for me introduced me to the concept of the Pomodoro Technique. In essence, you focus intensely for 25 minutes and then take five minutes off. Then you repeat this process, ideally, eight times. At the end, it's typical that putting periodic breaks into your working schedule will exponentially increase your output, and that's exactly what happened to me.

I was able to finish the term paper on Karl Marx well ahead of schedule and discovered what it felt like to turn tasks in ahead of time and actually sleep before they were due. This simple technique started me on the path to discovering what about human focus makes us want to procrastinate so much, and what we can do about it.

I was focused on focus and dug into the science of achievement, evolutionary biology, behavioral economics, and anything else you can think of. Focus is a product of our willpower and other subconscious drives, so you can imagine that just about every desire we have plays a role in it.

At least, that's the best way to approach it. You see, it's not always possible to just pull an all-nighter like I was known for in college. Real life doesn't give you that opportunity or liberty, so learning to focus is really learning the biggest ability of all—to achieve what you set your mind to. Getting more done in less time. Being able to achieve your goals.

When we think about what we want out of life, it's only made possible through focus and perhaps a small amount of luck. Focus is the end game for much of self-improvement, even though we might think of it in other names.

I've implemented every single one of the scientifically proven methods in this book myself to great results. Not every one stuck, but they all impacted me in some way. Best of all, you don't have to believe me—believe the research scientists who ran the research studies!

At work these days, people would never guess that I had a reputation for cutting it extremely close to deadlines. I find that with just a few of the focus techniques in this book, I can consistently work ahead of schedule. Of course, don't let them know that, because then I might get assigned more to do!

Best,

Peter

Chapter 1. Discipline and Willpower

When you think of the word *discipline*, what image comes to mind? Chances are good that you thought of something negative—being spanked or sent to your room as a child or receiving a warning for some infraction at work. Most people tend to think of discipline as a punishment, but in actuality, the definition refers to training that corrects, molds, or perfects mental capacity or moral character. True, many parents achieve this outcome by using various forms of punishment, so the negative association is well founded.

However, discipline is also a trait celebrated and revered in many circles, especially athletics. Any pro athlete will tell you that it takes discipline to make it in the majors. Michael Jordan, acknowledged as possibly the greatest basketball player of all time, once remarked that he wasn't out there sweating on the court three hours a day just to find out what it feels like to sweat. He understood the need to train his mind and his body to perform to the best of his ability, even on days when he would have preferred to stay in bed.

Willpower is a companion to discipline. It is the mindset of energetic determination that allows discipline to manifest. Many people view willpower as a mechanism of failure, because it is closely associated with avoiding temptation. At the end of a long work day, it's a lot easier to sit down and watch TV than to go for a run, but for those with a desire to optimize their health, the combination of discipline and willpower win out. More often than not, they find themselves lacing up their sneakers and heading out the door.

These two traits are what we aspire to because we tend to feel that we aren't doing as much as we can. In the face of hardship, simply not acting is the easiest path of all. But deep down, we realize that we simply aren't going to get what we want in life if we can't muster the will to do what we don't love from time to time. Indeed, on some level it comes to the costs (anything worth working hard for) being compared to the benefits (the hard work itself). Clearly these have cache when attempting to focus better on a task at hand.

Pushing the Boulder

Sometimes there's no way of avoiding a task, and you just have to grind through it. You hate it, it makes you miserable, and there's simply no spinning it into something positive. This is the reality-changing power of discipline and willpower, because it allows you to toil in the darkness despite any type of emotional objection. Tasks with no glory or redeeming qualities are inevitable; ditches must be dug by somebody, and sometimes you can't avoid it.

If you experience a lack of motivation or focus, discipline and willpower are effective substitutes for pushing past the misery. Like Sisyphus in the ancient Greek myth, cursed forever to roll a boulder uphill, sometimes a task feels endless. Many people, especially those in creative fields, believe that they must rely on motivation, inspiration, or their muse in order to create. That notion is dead wrong and generates a false narrative that leads people to sit around waiting for something that rarely, if ever, appears. During those periods when the muse is silent, when there is no flash of creative genius, true artists rely on discipline to move past the block and keep the work flowing.

Prolific author Stephen King recalls a time when he was affected by writer's block during college. He ceased work on a particular novel because it wasn't quite right and he didn't know how to fix it. That led to a four-month period during which he drank beer and watched soap operas. Disgusted by his lack of motivation, King decided to write something every day, even if it was garbage. He just set the goal of writing a few pages every day, something that at the time took tremendous willpower.

Eventually, inspired by the continuous soapy tragedies unfolding before him, King finally hit on a solution—throw *more* problems at his characters, not fewer. He decided to stop trying to patch up the bad with the good. Instead, he chose to make it worse for his characters and then sit back and watch them extricate themselves from the mess. It worked like a charm. As soon as he allowed the characters to act naturally instead of imposing his will upon them, the story unfolded before him and he was able to finish the book. All he needed to do was put his pen to the paper and *act* in order for the boulder to finally start budging.

We tend to want instant gratification for our efforts, and when it doesn't come, we feel deflated and like our efforts were in vain. This, of course, is why crash diets will always have a place in people's hearts. However, the concept of delayed gratification is far more effective.

Discipline, Willpower, and Delayed Gratification

Self-control (self-discipline) is directly linked to our ability to handle stress, plan ahead, and remain focused.

A famous study by Walter Mischel, Ph.D., dubbed the "marshmallow test," demonstrates these links quite clearly. A preschooler was presented with a plate of treats, such as marshmallows, and told that they must wait before indulging. Before leaving the room, the researcher would tell the child that if they could wait until the researcher returned they, could have two marshmallows, but if they were unable to wait, they could ring a bell and the researcher would return, but they would only be allowed a single treat. Their willpower was being tested through delayed gratification.

When Mischel revisited his test subjects as teenagers, he discovered that the children who had held out for a double treat as preschoolers were already exhibiting more potential than their impatient peers. They tended to score higher on the SAT, and their parents had positive things to say when asked to describe their children. The parents were more likely to describe them as having greater self-control in frustrating situations, as being able to concentrate without becoming distracted and as exhibiting a greater ability to plan ahead—glowing reviews for any teen! The parents had full confidence that their children would become responsible and capable adults.

These same subjects were revisited a third time, during their 40s, and the results of the third trial were striking. Instead of marshmallows, the researchers used a laboratory task known to validate self-control in adults. Remarkably, the subjects' willpower strength had endured across the decades. As you might expect, those who were unable to tolerate delayed gratification as children scored poorly on similar self-control tasks as adults. And as you may also suspect, these same adults hadn't fared as well in life as their more patient counterparts. In fact, they exhibited reduced academic attainment and had higher BMI scores (a measure of body fat) in their later lives. This decades-long study demonstrates that impulse control can be a relatively accurate marker for success in a variety of life situations.

What does the marshmallow test tell us about our ability to deal with stress, to plan ahead, and to remain focused?

Since the researchers followed the same subjects for roughly four decades, measuring the same qualities repeatedly, we can extrapolate their findings across the general population to arrive at some universal assumptions about human behavior. Our willpower largely remains constant throughout our lifetime. The children who exhibited impatience and were unwilling to wait for a greater reward went on to indulge their impulses throughout later life, resulting in greater weight gain and a reduced level of education. (Presumably they did not have the patience to endure advanced instruction beyond high school.) Those who showed early promise continued to display those characteristics well into adulthood.

Delayed gratification is the act of foregoing distractions, temptations, and other shiny objects in lieu of focusing on what's in front of you or on your to-do list. Playing video games is the immediate marshmallow that sabotages the rest of your focus efforts.

The Future Self Dilemma

In studies conducted at Harvard University, Jason Mitchell discovered that self-discipline is inherently difficult to maintain because it's challenging for people to envision the reward that their "future self" will receive. This sounds very similar to delayed gratification.

The goal of discipline *today* is to receive a direct benefit in the *future*. Practicing the piano for half an hour each day not only validated your parents' expense for piano lessons, but it prepared you for that all-important recital, making you look like a rock star in comparison to the humiliated kids who didn't practice. Every single afternoon practice session was painful, but when the time came to perform, you were glad you stuck with it. Unfortunately, though, the notion of future self, which is closely tied to planning ahead, is not realistic for many people.

During one study, participants underwent brain scans while thinking about one of three subjects: their current self, a specific celebrity, or themselves in 10 years. Surprisingly, the scans of participants thinking about the celebrity or thinking about themselves in a decade were nearly identical. This indicates that while we may be familiar with the subjects, we don't attach personal significance to them. They are not relevant to us in the current moment. In other words, we view our future self with the same detachment as someone we don't personally know.

The phenomena of detachment from our future self may explain why people procrastinate. We certainly won't use the same care or scrutiny on others as we might ourselves, so this behavioral tendency is another aspect of human nature that sabotages our focus. In our minds, we can offload unpleasant tasks to be handled by our future self because we don't connect the consequences with our current lives. This is a mind game that often leads us to choose behaviors that seem self-destructive or counterproductive, like skipping the gym for the fourth day in a row because it's raining. Rationally, it doesn't make sense, but we justify it by saying our willpower is weak, when in reality we are simply unable to visualize the long-term consequences and connect them with ourselves today.

Frequently, the outcome of this faulty reasoning is a self-induced crisis. We postpone an activity until the last possible moment and then in a frenzy of anxiety bear down and power through it. Although there are people who work well (and creatively) under pressure, for the most part, we don't do our best work while under the influence of extreme stress. Crash dieting is a classic example of the dangers of disconnecting from our future self. The cheesecake that is irresistible in the moment seems harmless enough, but when we are two weeks away from fitting into that bridesmaid dress, suddenly we regret that decision, decide that all food is the enemy, and starve until the zipper slides all the way to the top.

Methods for Increasing Self-Discipline

Given all of our inborn obstacles, the question becomes, can self-discipline and willpower be learned? Can we really learn how to just grind our teeth together and work like a machine when the time comes? The answer is: maybe.

The key seems to be awareness. A joint study conducted by the Hong Kong University of Science and Chicago University demonstrated that understanding *why* a specific action was chosen helped boost self-discipline. Participants were asked to describe a time when they resisted temptation; they were immediately thereafter offered an indulgence and 70% gave in. But when another group was asked to explain *why* they had resisted a temptation, 69% were able to turn down the indulgence. They placed strong emotional value on resistance and acknowledged a benefit from avoiding a previous temptation, so merely being aware of the reason for resistance significantly reinforced their self-discipline.

Repetition (coupled with awareness) seems to be the most effective strategy in improving self-discipline. Creating new and positive habits is essential to improving self-discipline. Consider this study at Northwestern University—40 adults in romantic relationships were divided into three groups: one group was asked to use their non-dominant hand to brush their teeth; another group was asked to begin saying "yes" instead of "yeah"; and the third group (control group) was not given any instructions.

After two weeks, both the teeth-brushing group and the yes group reported a reduced tendency toward becoming irritable with their partners. There was no change in the control group. What's the significance? Any activity that causes the brain to pause and choose a different tactic disrupts the usual thought patterns, creating greater awareness. This new awareness provides an opportunity to break the customary cycle of action/reaction. The brain spontaneously begins to apply this pause across all its decision-making processes, which makes adopting the harder thing (like saying yes instead of yeah) a deliberate choice. We attach a greater emotional reward to the selection, and thus we begin choosing the newer, more rewarding behavior.

In practical terms, it is difficult to "think about thinking," but increased awareness of your current actions don't have to come from you. In theory, what you need is a floating arrow to follow you around and poke you when you're not on task, and there are multiple ways to create that feeling. They can come from reminders you put around your home or workspace, phone alarms, or friends who will contact to keep you accountable.

Discipline and willpower—they can be a potent combination, as long as we understand how they work together. Overcoming the restrictions of future-self beliefs is mandatory for making discipline effective today. If we don't believe that the satisfaction we delay today will bring us benefit in the future, then we won't be willing to make the sacrifice. Life becomes focused on one marshmallow now instead of a double reward later. But when the practice of awareness is added to the mix, things start to get interesting. Now our brain is repeatedly pausing to assess our actions, and we are reinforcing our self-discipline by making active choices. We learn that we can do the hard thing with relative ease, and that the more often we make that choice, the easier it becomes. That is when our discipline and willpower receive a boost, and even without strong motivation, we can push through the impossible.

Chapter 2. Goals

Learning to set—and achieve—goals will be a tremendous boost to improving your focus. Many people shy away from goal-setting because they erroneously believe that it's difficult and time-consuming or that it's simply a complete waste of time. In actuality, setting goals can be simple, and once you've accomplished a few, the feeling of success can become addictive in driving you toward more and better. Achieving goals is a great motivator because it offers you an opportunity to celebrate your success and reward yourself for a job well done.

Specifically, goals provide structure and frame for your focus to take root and bloom.

Daydreams vs. Goals

There's an old saying: you can't hit a target you can't see. This statement is especially true when applied to the concept of goal-setting. If you have a goal, say losing five pounds by the end of the month, but you have no plan or action steps for reaching that goal, then you are not likely to hit the target. In reality, you haven't set a goal at all—you simply have a dream that is vague and hazy and thus will never be reached.

A study conducted by Gail Matthews at California's Dominican University demonstrates the effectiveness of making goals concrete. She requested that her study participants put their personal goal in writing and keep it where they could see it often, at least daily. She discovered that her subjects were 42% more likely to achieve their goal when it was written down. The act of writing the words cements the purpose in our minds, sort of a mental "carved in stone." It's much more difficult to cheat when it's staring you in the face. In essence, when a goal is spoken out loud and made to be "real," it can no longer hide.

Setting a goal brings clarity to our desires and gives direction to our thoughts and actions, even when we aren't consciously focusing on it. Our intent remains active in the back of the mind, influencing our choices and setting us up for success. For example, if you were hungry and you saw your weight loss goal stuck to the refrigerator door as you went in for a snack, it would likely prompt you to choose a piece of fruit or a hard-boiled egg instead of a handful of cookies. In the moment, you may not be conscious of the reason for your choice, but your subconscious is nudging you toward success.

Matthews further found that when her subjects shared their goal and kept their supportive friends updated on their progress, they did even better. Setting a goal, writing it down, and making it public requires us to be accountable. Most people don't like to disappoint others (or themselves), so having a small measure of accountability acts as a motivator to stick with the program. This concept is the foundation for programs like Weight Watchers, where progress tracking and sincere support are key factors in reaching a weight management goal. Weight Watchers also rewards members for their progress by celebrating achievements publicly, thereby reinforcing positive behavior and providing incentive for members just beginning their weight loss journey.

When you speak a goal into reality, it becomes something that follows you and begs to be addressed. It is added to your mental (or real) to-do list and cannot be brushed off as a fantasy or daydream anymore.

Create a Positive Environment

Even with our stated goal in hand, most of us have the freedom to make a wide range of choices at any given moment. This can wreak havoc with achieving goals, because researchers have found that we often make decisions based on our immediate environment.

Our *default decision* is usually whatever happens to be the easiest option, so make them support your goals. If you keep your smartphone next to your bed, checking email or social media as soon as you wake up is likely to be your default decision. Keeping alcohol in the house is likely to make drinking consistently a default decision. Therefore, in light of meeting our goals, it makes sense to set up our environment to support achievement.

Using the example of losing five pounds, how can we set up our immediate environment in a way that supports our goal? We can stock the kitchen with a variety of portion-controlled healthy snacks so we're ready when a snack attack strikes. We can spend a weekend afternoon preparing nourishing meals for the week ahead so we don't end up making a last-minute fast food run because there's "nothing good" in the house. Placing the dog's leash in plain sight serves as a reminder for us to get out and get moving instead of plopping down on the couch with a bowl of buttery popcorn. Placing a set of hand weights next to the TV reminds us that we can multitask by doing bicep curls while watching our favorite show.

The same kind of environmental changes can be made at our workplace. Ridding our workstation of calorie-laden snacks and replacing them with nuts, protein bars, or fresh, crunchy veggies will help keep us from feeling deprived. Taking a walk around the block at break time is a more soul-satisfying choice than taking a walk to the vending machine. And the old standby, brown bagging a healthy lunch, will not only save on unnecessary calories, but will save a few bucks as well. Each one of these small, simple tweaks to our usual routine makes a positive impact and moves us in the direction of success.

Whatever your goals are, there are at least five ways you can tailor your environment to assist with them, whether it be through reminders (posters, alarms), making actions more difficult or easy (only healthy food, a "no elevators" rule), or switching environments altogether (going to the office, getting a desk too small to hold snacks).

Set a Realistic Time Frame

Turning a daydream into a goal doesn't have to be a long, drawn-out undertaking. In fact, the quicker you can get it done, the better. Accomplishing a series of small goals reassures us that we are both competent and capable. But sometimes, especially when we feel unsure of our ability, we con ourselves into believing that a goal will require much more time than is realistic. That's when Parkinson's Law comes into play.

British historian Cyril Parkinson developed his theory during a stint with the British Civil Service. He observed that as the bureaucracy expanded it became less and less efficient, leading him to postulate that "Work expands so as to fill the time available for its completion." In other words, the more time you allot for a task, the longer it will require.

Parkinson found that even a series of simple tasks were perceived to increase in complexity when an excessive amount of time was allotted for completion. He further observed that even though there might not be enough actual work to fill the time, anxiety and tension about having to do the work expanded significantly. A great amount of energy was spent worrying about the work, not actually doing the work! By contrast, when a shorter amount of time was prescribed, efficiency increased and tasks were completed with far less stress.

Building on Parkinson's Law, a study of college students found that those who imposed strict deadlines on themselves for completing assignments consistently performed better than those who gave themselves an excessive amount of time and those who set no limits at all. Why? The artificial limitations they had set for their work caused them to be far more efficient than their counterparts. They didn't spend a lot of time worrying about the assignments because they didn't give themselves the time to indulge. They got to work, finished the projects, and moved on. They also didn't have time to ruminate on what ultimately didn't matter—a very common type of subtle procrastination. They were able to subconsciously focus on only the elements that mattered in completing the assignment.

Former President Barack Obama was famous for self-imposing deadlines during his term in office. As the leader of the free world, he felt forced to work as efficiently as possible. He even went so far as to "routinize" himself when it came to making decisions about everyday occurrences. He told *Vanity Fair Magazine*, "You'll see I only wear gray or blue suits. I'm trying to pare down decisions. Because I have too many other [important] decisions to make. You need to focus your decision-making energy . . . You can't be going through the day distracted by trivia." Instead of allotting time in the mornings to dress, he gave himself a binary choice with (likely) a 30-second time allotment.

Obama understood that he had a finite amount of energy and set a goal to concentrate on the things he considered important while eliminating distractions.

Effectiveness goes hand-in-hand with efficiency and speed. By limiting time frames and setting up routines, we can increase our speed, but swiftness does not ensure accuracy. Let's consider a surgeon—he is highly skilled, the finest knee surgeon in the country. His prep team comes in ahead of him to make sure the OR is sterile, to set up the necessary instruments and supplies, and to anesthetize the patient. They carefully clean and prep the patient's right knee for the first incision. Unfortunately, it is the left knee that requires surgery. So regardless of the surgeon's skill, the operation will not be effective since it was performed on the wrong body part. In this instance, streamlining the process may have led to efficiency, (doing things right) but not effectiveness (doing the right things). Inefficient and ineffective processes are costly both in terms of dollars and reliability.

That's why learning to set SMART goals can help prevent failure and keep us motivated.

SMART Goals

SMART is an acronym for a system that can eliminate daydreams and get you focused on setting specific, attainable goals. By asking the right questions and following the SMART system, you can set goals that will inevitably explode your focus.

S = Specific

We already know that a goal has a specific focus, or it is just a daydream. In order to get focused, ask the following questions: who, what, where, when, why, and which.

Who is involved? *What* do I want to achieve? *Where* will the action(s) be performed? *When* will I do it or how long will it take? *Why* do I want to do this (list purpose or benefits of goal)? *Which* methods or tools will I use (list requirements and/or restrictions)? Identifying the answers to these questions will narrow the focus of the dream and outline the goal. The more details the better, as it will make the goal planning more realistic and account for everything that could detract from it.

M = Measurable

Establish criteria for measuring your progress toward the goal by asking *how*. How much? How many? How long? How do I know when the goal is achieved? What can you look at on a daily basis to understand that you are indeed moving forward and not regressing or remaining stagnant? Having something to measure will allow you to know whether changes need to be made in your goal approach.

A = Attainable

By establishing goals that are important to you, your mind moves in a direction that allows you to attain them. You give yourself permission to develop the attitudes, abilities, skills, and financial capacity necessary to reach the goal. Your self-image changes, and you begin to see yourself as capable and worthy of the goal. You may become aware of previously overlooked opportunities and a period of growth begins.

R = Realistic

You must be willing and able to work toward a goal for it to be considered realistic. A higher, seemingly harder goal is often easier to reach than a moderate or low goal, because the challenge serves as a stronger motivator. Start small and set milestones instead of one large goal. Having only one large goal can be extremely disheartening because any progress you make can seem insignificant in the grand scheme of things. Small goals will make you feel achievement and real progress on a daily basis.

T = Timely

As with the successful college students who imposed deadlines for themselves in completing work, being timely instills a sense of urgency. It makes you get off your butt and do something. Losing those five pounds by the end of the month requires more immediate effort than losing five pounds someday. **T** can also stand for "**Tangible**," meaning that you can experience it with one of your senses. It is much easier to be realistic and specific when you can see, hear, smell, touch, or taste it.

The process of setting and attaining realistic goals is not mysterious or out of reach of the average person. It's easy to get out of the dream zone by setting yourself up for success—put your goal in writing, share it with others, and allow them to support and encourage you. A little accountability will help you maintain focus.

If the going gets tough and you find it difficult to maintain motivation, take a step back and reassess. Have you set a realistic time frame? Don't forget that *efficient* is not the same as *effective*, so make sure you are doing the right things, not just doing things right. What about creating a positive environment? Have you unwittingly undermined yourself by stashing a bag of M&Ms in your desk drawer? Try working through the SMART goal system and see if you've actually defined your goal.

And remember that it's important to reward yourself when you get there. Slipping easily into those previously snug-fitting jeans is cause for celebration. Make sure to congratulate yourself for a job well done and acknowledge what it took to get there. By praising yourself for achievement, you keep building the foundation for continued success.

Chapter 3. Procrastination

Procrastination is the tendency to postpone tasks that cause us discomfort in favor of activities that bring us pleasure or excitement. It can last nearly forever, and we can also trick ourselves into thinking that we *aren't* procrastinating by cleaning our bathrooms or vacuuming.

Quick quiz: in the next 15 minutes, would you rather eat a pizza or do your tax return?

You get the point. Procrastination is an issue of self-control in which we are tempted to seek short-term relief by avoiding stressful or boring tasks. Unfortunately, this behavior often results in some type of crisis in the aftermath of our avoidance. No matter how efficient and goal-driven you are, procrastination creeps in when you aren't looking, and BAM! There you are, playing Candy Crush on your smartphone as the hours tick away and the research for your doctoral thesis sits untouched next to your dormant computer. What happened to your focus and your goal of finishing on time?

So knowing that task avoidance may cause us to have to work twice as hard to get something done in less time, or that we may need to do damage control as a result of not finishing, what exactly triggers us to delay activities that are actually important to us?

It would be impossible to quantify all the reasons for procrastination, but researchers have defined three procrastinator "types." *Arousal procrastinators* get a thrill from waiting until the last moment—"I work best under pressure." *Avoidant procrastinators* are unwilling to face an unpleasant task—"I'd just rather not right now..." *Indecisive procrastinators* are intimidated by their task and frequently don't know how to start—"I could do it like this, but also that other way. I'll have to research and plan some more."

Any of those sound familiar? That's because according to Srini Pillay, an assistant clinical professor of psychiatry at Harvard Medical School, most of us are some combination of all three.

Frank Lloyd Wright, the prolific and groundbreaking architect, was known to procrastinate, particularly on large-scale projects. One of his most famous designs, the private home known as Fallingwater, which has been designated a National Historic Landmark, was conceived and drawn up in one morning. Wright had accepted the commission months previously but hadn't done a thing. To his surprise, the client telephoned one Sunday morning saying he was nearby on business and would be stopping in around lunchtime to inspect the plans. An arousal-type procrastinator, the adrenaline rush provided by the client's announcement was enough to propel Wright's creativity into high gear, and he produced the plans for a structure that now appears on the Smithsonian's list of "28 Places to Visit Before You Die." It's a risky game, but some people do indeed rely on their abilities to finish things rather quickly.

Colonel Johann Rall provides us with an excellent example of an avoidant procrastinator.

The German commander of Hessian troops at the Battle of Trenton, Colonel Rall was playing cards when a messenger arrived with a note revealing that General George Washington was crossing the Delaware River in preparation for engaging Rall in battle. Messengers generally did not represent good news during the Revolutionary War, so Rall pocketed the note without opening it in favor of finishing his card game. Washington's troops attacked the next morning, capturing most of the Hessians—a turning point in the war for independence. Rall was wounded in the brief battle and died later that day, the unopened missive still tucked in his pocket. When we try to avoid a small annoyance, it can quickly snowball.

Canadian author Margaret Atwood, famous for her novel *The Handmaid's Tale*, is a self-proclaimed indecisive procrastinator. Throughout her 50-year career, she has churned out 14 novels, 16 volumes of poetry, eight children's books, and countless other written works. Despite her prodigious productivity, by her own admission Atwood spends her mornings "procrastinating and worrying, and then plunges into the manuscript in a frenzy of anxiety around 3:00 p.m."

It is worth noting that although procrastination is generally viewed as a negative attribute, it can prove beneficial, as demonstrated by both Lloyd Wright and Atwood. Although they represent different types of procrastinators, as creatives, their resourcefulness reaches its peak when anxiety reaches critical mass. While not a highly recommended method for achieving the ultimate in artistic expression, it certainly works for the select few. For the rest of us, procrastination creates the dark cloud hanging over our heads.

Battle of the Brains

If you've been mentally kicking yourself for your bad habit (or if your significant other has been doing it for you), you'll be pleased to know that it's not all your fault. You are not just a lazy bum—physiologically speaking, your brain is at war with itself when it comes to procrastination. Our brains are wired to prefer pleasure over pain, and nature has developed an ingenious system for coaxing us to give in. The battle raging between the strong, dominant limbic system and the weaker prefrontal cortex commences unrestrained from the moment we are born.

Our limbic system, which controls mood and instinct, is a dominant part of the brain and operates 24/7. It helps keep us safe by causing us to move away from danger, such as pulling our fingers away from a candle flame. Basic emotions including fear, anger, and pleasure originate here, and certain "drives," including libido, are also controlled by the limbic system.

A limbic region known as the amygdala, the brain's pleasure center, is largely responsible for the procrastination response. By constantly urging us to seek pleasure over pain, the amygdala rewards us with a jolt of dopamine (the pleasure chemical produced by our bodies) whenever we are confronted with an unpleasant task. It tries to entice us to go with the flow and stay away from anything difficult or painful. In fact, it takes only 1/32 of a second for the amygdala to recognize displeasure and "correct" it.

By contrast, the limbic system's weaker cousin, the prefrontal cortex, takes a full three seconds to react to stimuli. The prefrontal cortex is the area of the brain that assimilates information and makes decisions. The time lag between the firing of the amygdala and the engagement of the prefrontal cortex explains why we are more likely to comply with our indulgent impulses. Unlike the amygdala, connecting with the prefrontal cortex is not an automatic process. We must actively engage the prefrontal cortex, which then helps us focus and eventually pushes us to complete a job or task.

An interesting aside, scientists have identified the existence of the prefrontal cortex as the key brain function that separates humans from animals. It is our ability to operate outside the realm of instinct that allows us self-determination instead of simply the animal ability to survive. Although our lack of motivation may appear sloth-like to some, we are indeed separated from the animal kingdom by our ability to set and achieve goals and our determination to remain focused on the things that are important to us—even if we have a difficult time getting started!

So on a neurobiological level, procrastination appears to be instinctually driven by a desire to avoid the negative emotions associated with fear or failure. The "fight-or-flight" response, commonly linked to a perceived threat to our survival, has also been linked to task avoidance and procrastination. When we begin to feel overwhelmed by a situation or a series of tasks, the amygdala tries to protect us from feelings of anxiety, panic, or self-doubt by inducing a similar fight-or-flight response.

During an episode of anxiety or fear, the amygdala releases a flood of the hormone adrenaline. Adrenaline makes it possible to exit a difficult situation swiftly, either by running or fighting. It's the brain chemical that gives parents the super strength to rescue their trapped toddler from beneath the wheels of a car. Unfortunately, a flood of adrenaline can blunt the reactions of the prefrontal cortex, making it more difficult to make rational decisions and leaving you vulnerable to additional impulsive emotional responses from the amygdala.

The combination of dopamine and adrenaline is the one-two punch that reinforces procrastinating behaviors.

When pain or displeasure is perceived, the amygdala tries to persuade us with a shot of dopamine and then follows it up with adrenaline to get us moving in the direction of a more enjoyable activity. This is the reason you sometimes find yourself engaged in "productive procrastination"—alphabetizing your CD collection when you really need to be finishing those reports for work. We avoid the most important (scary) task by replacing it with a different (less intimidating) activity. We are then able to justify our actions by displaying tangible results.

It would appear that nature has doomed us from the start by pitting our instinct against our more honorable desires to remain focused and accomplish our goals. It's not a fail-safe system, however. Human ingenuity has found a number of workarounds, and through sheer grit and determination, will probably identify more in the future. Without further delay, let's take a look at how we can overcome procrastination.

Winning the Procrastination Battle

Knowing that our own brain is against us, how do we get off the couch and get busy?

Researcher Kenneth McGraw has found that the biggest impediment to success is simply getting started. Our tendency to procrastinate on large or intimidating projects is reinforced by our imagination. We visualize the worst parts of the task, adding layers of emotion each time we picture ourselves performing it, and that makes it easier to delay getting started. But we can overcome this inertia by implementing the 10-minute rule.

The rule is very simple: commit to starting the project and sticking with it for 10 minutes.

The goal is to achieve a small success and build upon it. When you've been active with a project for 10 minutes, momentum begins to build, and that momentum will drive you forward for another 10 minutes, and so on. You may start out by making your bed and then decide to vacuum the bedroom as well. Since you've got the vacuum cleaner out, you may as well do the living room and the den—before you know it, you've accomplished the goal of straightening the house and you can give yourself a pat on the back.

If you find you are still having difficulty getting started at the end of 10 minutes, disengage from the activity and do something physical for 10 minutes—take a walk, do some yoga poses, play with your dog. Give your brain time to relax and come to grips with the idea that you are *doing this*, but don't fill it with competing projects. Then go back to your task, set the timer for 10 minutes, and get to work. Chances are good that you'll achieve a significant measure of success the second time around.

It seems that if we can move our conscious mind past the initial freak-out phase of tackling a project, our subconscious takes over, devising ways to help us stay focused on reaching the goal. Baby steps could be crucial. After we've defined our overarching goal, we can learn to sidestep the overwhelming fear that paralyzes us, the insecurity that whispers, "You aren't good enough. You can't do this. It's too big." That's why breaking down the goal into a series of smaller tasks and completing those tasks one by one gives us the self-confidence to keep moving forward. Soon our mindset shifts to, "This isn't so hard. Look how far you've come! You've got this!"

Self-control is the key to mastering procrastination. Understanding that we are wired to shy away from tasks that are intimidating or complex is the first step in overcoming our natural tendencies. Developing the willingness to commit to a task for 10 minutes can be a valuable deterrent to either giving up or getting sucked into other "productive" procrastination activities. Building the momentum that will carry us through to the completion of the task is crucial, for it is this small measure of success that spurs us on. And knowing when it's time to take a break, to give our brain time to regroup, is vital. The trick is to just get started.

Chapter 4. Energy

There are so many factors that contribute to maintaining and optimizing our ability to focus, but none is more basic than managing our energy levels. If you have energy, you can try to focus and work; if you don't have energy, you will be stuck in bed eating ice cream. It's that simple—energy is the most important part of maximizing your focus. Just as a track athlete needs adequate sleep and nutrition before a race, you need energy for powerful focus.

From a biological standpoint, each person has a finite amount of energy available on a daily basis, so understanding your body's rest and wake cycles can help you determine how to maximize productivity. Paying attention to your own natural rhythms is essential to pinpointing the best hours of the day to accomplish your desired tasks.

You know from personal experience that your energy level varies throughout the day. No one operates at a high energy level 100% of the time. You've probably experienced the mid-afternoon food coma, which usually occurs a couple hours after lunch. This can be quite problematic if you are at work where your boss is telling you to churn out a report but your body is telling you to take a nap. It is possible to circumvent the body's natural rhythms through use of stimulants, such as caffeine, but inevitably, the artificially high-energy period is followed by a crash when the body insists on rest.

Energy management is about understanding how your body works and taking advantage of it instead of falling prey to it.

Circadian Science

This natural energy cycle is called the *circadian rhythm*.

Researchers have long been interested in the rest/activity cycle of the human body, so there is a large quantity of scientific research detailing this very intimate sequence. As an outcome of his pioneering sleep research, where he identified the presence and importance of rapid eye movement (REM) sleep, Neil Kleitman discovered that the body generally operates in 90-minute cycles, moving progressively through periods of higher and lower alertness. Understanding the circadian rhythm can help us predict how a person might function during a typical 24-hour period. The sequence applies whether we are awake or asleep, and we can use this information to our advantage by scheduling tasks to coincide with our own peak performance times.

As we move through a typical day, it takes a few hours after waking to reach our peak levels of energy and alertness. For most people, the late morning hours, after 10:00 a.m., represent the highest period of mental sharpness and focus. This is the best time to begin tasks that require heavy cognitive input—scheduling, mathematical equations, persuasive writing. Focusing on intense tasks during the late morning hours takes advantage of your fully awake brain, increasing productivity by syncing with your natural rhythm. Tony Schwartz, writing for the *Harvard Business Review*, reports that Kleitman found that working intensely for 90 minutes, followed by a rest period of no more than 15–20 minutes, is the ideal sequence for optimum mental performance. This follows the rhythm we see in sleep.

At the end of an intense 90-minute work period, details Schwartz, we begin relying on stress hormones for energy. Suffering from overload, the prefrontal cortex begins to shut down, and we move into fight-or-flight syndrome. We may attempt to override the body's signals by fueling ourselves with caffeine and sugar, which buys us a little more productive work time, but in the end, our focus and concentration still suffer. Research from both Peretz Lavie and the US Army Research Institute back up these findings, stating unequivocally that following our natural circadian rhythms of 90-minute work periods followed by a short rest allows us to maintain stronger focus and higher energy levels throughout the day.

The point here is to listen to your body. It is telling you exactly how it prefers to function during sleep, and it should be no different when awake. When you sit down to work, you have a ticking time bomb of 90 minutes before you lose peak effectiveness and focus. Of course, some people may be less or more talented in this field, but your focus isn't limitless. This is also why it's so important to get rid of distractions so they are not allowed to eat into your 90-minute period of peak performance.

An interesting example of this work cycle is borne out by a study of the practice techniques of professional violinists. The most common regimen for top flight violinists is a

90-minute block of intense practice followed immediately by a 15-minute break. This is a standard they have developed out of thousands of hours of practice and what they feel helped improve the most. Certainly, if world-class musicians benefit from arranging their time into 90-minute cycles, we should follow their cue and become the virtuosos of our own office!

The Pomodoro Technique

Taking this idea to the next level, entrepreneur Francesco Cirillo developed the Pomodoro Technique in the late 1980s to supercharge his productivity. Jokingly named Pomodoro after the tomato-shaped timer he used to track his work periods, Cirillo trained his brain to focus for short, intense periods that helped him remain consistently productive. He followed each work period (a Pomodoro) with a short, scheduled break that kept him motivated and bolstered creativity. The technique is not only effective, but incredibly simple: set a timer for 25 minutes and start working. When the timer goes off, take a short break (5–10 minutes) and then begin the next Pomodoro. After four Pomodoros, take a longer rest period, usually 30 minutes.

Cirillo notes that it's important to honor the Pomodoro. If you are interrupted for more than a couple of minutes, you have a choice to make—either save your work and end that Pomodoro or postpone the distraction. If you are 15 minutes into a Pomodoro and the boss calls you into a meeting, you know you won't be completing that 25-minute cycle, so save your work and begin a new Pomodoro after the meeting ends. If, however, you receive a phone call and have the ability to handle the business at a later time by returning the call, you can go ahead and complete your Pomodoro.

Either way, you have respected the Pomodoro and your productivity shouldn't suffer. It's a short version of adhering to your circadian tendencies.

Fatigue and Creativity

Soon after lunch, our energy levels begin to decline.

According to Christopher Barnes writing in the *Harvard Business Review*, your turkey sandwich isn't to blame (although your daily cycles can be affected by a wide variety of stimuli, including the type of food you eat). Our body's energy naturally dips somewhere between 2:00 and 3:00 p.m., possibly because we are at the midpoint of our wake cycle. For thousands of years, humans have rested during the afternoon (think the Spanish concept of the midday siesta), and it's only been since the Industrial Revolution imposed an emphasis on mass productivity that we have begun to eliminate this critical period of rest.

Ironically, our productivity still lags during the afternoon despite our modern conveniences, so we haven't achieved very much except to make ourselves cranky!

Although our productivity may wane during the mid-afternoon slump, our creativity frequently soars during this period. Brain fatigue appears to free up non-linear thinking, allowing you to venture outside the box and seek more creative solutions for problems you haven't been able to solve. In a 2011 study, more than 400 students were asked to work on a series of problems that required either analytical or novel thinking. The results showed that creative performance was best at non-peak times of the day—in other words, when they were tired.

Even when you feel like you aren't accomplishing anything, your brain is still busy, and you may be the beneficiary of that background work when you sit down for your next work session.

The Sleep Cycle

Once we hit that afternoon dip, our energy levels begin rising again, and we generally hit our second peak around 6:00 p.m. This is a period of high activity for most people, when we accomplish tasks that require stamina, such as exercising, housekeeping, playing with our kids or pets, etc. As the evening wears on, our energy diminishes, leading into the sleep cycle.

On average, most people sleep seven to eight hours per night. Given that we have 24 hours each day, that means sleep takes up roughly one-third of our time. The deepest part of sleep, known as REM sleep, occurs toward the end of the sleep cycle, and that is the time when our brains are most actively dreaming and when memory consolidation transpires. Studies have shown that lack of REM sleep impairs the ability to learn complex tasks and that children have far longer REM periods than adults.

This stands to reason, as we spend the early years of our lives absorbing the life lessons we need in order to survive. In essence, the brains of sleeping children are busy processing and assimilating their daily experiences, storing this information for future use.

The typical circadian pattern is very common, but individuals may exhibit significant differences. Sometimes the rhythm is shifted toward a specific time of day. Morning people, characterized as *larks*, tend to have energy peaks earlier in the day than the average person, while night people, called *owls*, are at their most effective after the sun goes down. Interestingly, there is a tendency to shift these patterns across the lifespan. Frequently, very young children tend to be larks, then shift into owls as adolescence occurs, and revert to larks once again as senior citizens.

The sleep/wake patterns of the youngest and oldest members of society are very similar, and it seems that our ancestors displayed wisdom in acknowledging this fact. For millennia, families existed in multi-generational households, where the needs of each life stage could be easily met through the process of communal care. Instead of this traditional model, we now see harried parents dropping off their toddlers at preschool and paying quick visits to their own parents at retirement homes after work. Could we as a society reduce our stress, improve our productivity, and sharpen our collective focus if we returned to a more traditional model of living? It's an interesting question to ponder.

<u>Take a Break</u>

The importance of taking breaks throughout the day can't be emphasized enough. Our brains are constantly bombarded by stimuli coming in from all of our senses. It's overwhelming and can cause our brains to undergo a type of paralysis where we simply can't make a rational decision. Taking time out to go for a walk, watch a cat video, or simply close your eyes for a few minutes is critical to our mental health.

Constant stimulation is registered by our brains as irrelevant—to the point where it is actually erased from our awareness. A prime example of this is having the television on while we go about our daily chores. Every once in a while, something catches our eye and we stop to focus on it, but for the most part, it's just white noise in the background. A study of computer users confirmed similar findings. When asked to perform the same activity repeatedly for an hour, the subjects became habituated to the movement, and after a while, the stimulus failed to register in a meaningful way. However, the subjects who performed the same activity, but with two brief breaks during the hour, performed consistently better. It seems fairly common sense, but too many people have the tendency to romanticize constant work and never taking breaks.

Conclusion: you need a break every now and then in order to see stimuli as "new" and be able to focus on it again. That stimuli could be something like the paper you are working on or song you are composing. When you've reached a point where everything seems the same and you need to read the same page five times to comprehend it, it's time for a break of a completely different activity.

Does Age Make a Difference?

Age may also make a difference.

Science has long held that fluid intelligence, defined as the ability to think quickly and recall information, peaks around age 20. However, brain age is far more complicated than previously perceived, and thoughts about fluid intelligence are changing. As reported in a 2015 study published in *Medical Xpress*, researchers identified approximately 30 subsets of intelligence, all of which peak at different times.

For example, raw processing speed peaks around the ages 18–20, which also happens to coincide with a high point in physical fitness. Notice that most professional athletes begin their careers (and set a lot of records) during this phase of their lives. They can train their bodies to maintain their physical skills, all the while sharpening their mental game, as short-term memory continues to improve until around the age of 35. Many retired athletes say that while they physically performed better at a younger age, they feel that they didn't develop a true understanding of their craft until they were a decade or more into their careers.

Significantly, skills such as reading other people's emotions peak much later, in our 40s and 50s. We find that people who engage in professions that require this type of analysis, such as therapists, social workers, and psychologists, tend to fall into the mid-life age group. As a society, we trust their experience and wisdom more than we would someone who was much younger. A young firefighter may be able to carry you down a ladder from the second floor, but his captain will be able to talk you off the ledge.

Personal energy management is as individual as a fingerprint. Your natural rhythms belong to you alone, and understanding your individual cycles can be a tremendous advantage in maintaining your personal focus and productivity. If you are a lark, it may be a best practice to get up and go for a run at first light and then dive into your work with gusto. Chances are good that you will get more done in the first half of the day than most people manage by sundown.

If, by contrast, you have difficulty getting started, employing a method like the Pomodoro Technique may be just what you need to fine tune your focus. This technique can be used by anyone at any age to squeeze the most productivity out of the waking hours. But don't forget the importance of taking a break (or two!). Down time is just as important to the brain as the ability to concentrate. Allowing our mental processes to roam frees our creativity and safeguards our mental health. It also allows us to come up with solutions to problems we just can't seem to solve with our analytical minds.

Finally, understanding that our energy and skills vary with age can help us make the most of our abilities. If you expect to bench press 250 pounds when you're 68, you may not have a realistic picture of your own capabilities. Likewise, if you expect to be taken seriously as a marriage counselor when you are 18, you may be surprised by the lack of clientele. Matching your productivity with your daily cycle is simply focusing on where you are in your life's journey, and that's appropriate at any age.

Chapter 5. Stress

"I'm so stressed out and my world is ending!" moans your coworker as she bangs her head on her cubicle wall. "The vending machine is out of Cheetos!"

You probably chuckled at that scenario, because we all know someone who over-dramatizes a relatively minor situation. However, the choice of words reveals a lot about the speaker. She feels burdened by the situation, as though the lack of Cheetos is a catastrophe. Since we don't know what else is going on in her life, it very well could be the last straw. But if you are like most people, you probably make a commiserating remark and go back to your own work.

Stress is probably one of the most over-used words in our collective vocabulary. It has become a popular excuse to explain away a lot of bad behavior, and thus it has been largely discounted in recent years. But stress—the psychological perception of danger and the body's response to it—is very real and should be taken seriously, not just in regards to your ability to focus. Learning to identify and manage stress appropriately will add years to your life and help improve your performance in a variety of life situations.

Yerkes Dodson Curve

Everyone has an optimal level of stress that encourages top performance. This level is achieved when you are alert and engaged, but not overly fearful. Let's say you are a contestant on a game show, and the subject for this round of questions is turtles. You are an expert on turtles, so you are excited and confident in your ability to answer the questions, and thus you are at your stress "sweet spot." But what if the subject was Greco-Roman wrestling? Would you have the same confidence, or would you begin to panic?

Finding the sweet spot is predicated on how physiologically aroused you are in the moment. If you are too aroused, you become stressed out, and you are bound to overthink the situation and mess up. If you aren't aroused enough (bored or uninterested), you aren't alert enough to pay attention because you simply don't care. The balance between these extremes is the sweet spot where you function at your best. You're a little bit nervous, but not too nervous. You're alert, but not overly stressed out.

The most famous method for measuring the optimal level of stress, the so-called sweet spot, was defined in 1908 by Robert Yerkes and John Dodson. They designed a graph in the shape of an upside-down U that demonstrates how our performance on a task will be poor when we are disengaged (uninterested), but as our arousal rises, our performance improves until it reaches the sweet spot—the Yerkes-Dodson Curve. Beyond that point, further arousal becomes a handicap. The stress becomes debilitating, and our performance suffers.

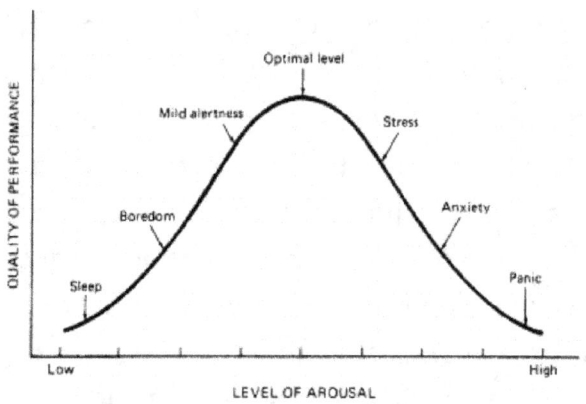

Image courtesy of ResearchGate

Imagine a golfer who has just hit a hole in one. That is an extremely difficult feat and not likely to be repeated during a single round. But he puts the pressure on himself to perform, feeling rigid and tense with the effort. Suddenly, he's incapable of making a three-foot putt, much less scoring another hole in one. He is too aroused, the alertness turns to great stress, and he chokes.

The goal in regards to focus is to find your optimal level of challenge where you don't feel bored but don't feel like you are tackling something impossible. This is what will keep you engaged, moving forward, and focused. You can do this in two ways.

First, you can manipulate how challenging tasks are to you. Of course, we don't always have the option of choosing what to work on, but you can change how challenging or easy a task is by giving yourself shorter or longer deadlines or ways to compete against yourself to give an otherwise easy task purpose and vigor. For instance, challenging yourself to write more or lose more weight in less time will create more *good* stress.

Second, you can design your work to alternate between easy and difficult tasks to keep you engaged and never too over- or underwhelmed. As mentioned, it's not often we can control that which we are trying to focus on, so at least we can spread out our stress strategically.

Your Brain on Stress

When you get frazzled, your brain immediately switches into crisis mode.

Control shifts from the executive functioning area in the prefrontal cortex to the more primitive mid-brain, engaging the instinctual fight-or-flight syndrome. It's an emergency response system that gives priority to speed (over rational thought) and knee-jerk responses (over creativity). Your body is literally trying to save your life, because the mid-brain cannot distinguish between an emotional crisis and a physical crisis. Self-preservation is its only function, and it does whatever it needs to do to make that transpire. If you encounter a lion in the wild, there's not typically time for thinking. Your body knows you just need to flee or fight and prepares itself accordingly.

A few different things happen in your body when you are in crisis mode.

First, your attention becomes focused on whatever is directly in front of you—the perceived threat. Your ability to focus otherwise is completely dashed. Peripheral vision greatly decreases, and your ability to absorb new information is restricted. As pressure intensifies, we are less able to retain information in working memory. We are unable to pay attention, and the ability to find flexible or creative solutions to our problem is virtually nonexistent. The further we dive into crisis mode, the deeper our descent into cognitive dysfunction, also known as brain fog.

Students frequently encounter brain fog. They may start out as bored or uninterested in the subject, say the War of 1812, and sit daydreaming in class. If their brains were imaged during this time, the scans would show a scattered pattern of activity spread throughout the brain, because their thoughts have little to do with the subject at hand. They are experiencing purely random thoughts—a trip to the mall, the upcoming Friday night football game, what to have for lunch.

Then the teacher announces that there will be a pop quiz at the end of the period, and suddenly the pattern changes, because motivation increases and they become engaged with the subject. A challenge has been issued, and brain activity rises to new heights of efficiency. They become focused and their cognitive abilities increase as the students attempt to meet the demand. For some, the challenge will come too late, and they will remain mired in crisis mode, too stressed out to focus. But for others, the challenge will propel them to their sweet spot, resulting in superior work.

Sweet Spot Corollary

An offshoot of the Yerkes-Dodson Curve states that certain tasks may be better suited to different levels of arousal. For example, we experience an adrenaline rush when we are stressed, but the resulting state of mind is more appropriate to the football field than the classroom. Tasks that are intellectually demanding seem to progress more smoothly when we aren't agitated and are more able to concentrate. If you're overly aroused, you might do better with physically demanding tasks—indeed, this just might be where the myths of the mothers with superhuman strength pulling cars off their children come from. If you are under-aroused, you are able to think more clearly without stress or pressure weighing down on you. The trick is to push ourselves to the sweet spot, presenting a challenge but not demanding too much.

Can we design our work or tasks to operate according to this theory? We can never anticipate all the surprises that life throws at us, but we can deal wisely with known factors. If you have something that requires intellectual power, you better work ahead of schedule; if you have a task that requires massive human strength, you might actually be better off procrastinating a bit. Maintain your optimal output and focus in this way.

For instance, if we have a large presentation at the office and we have two weeks to prepare, we can make a list of all the tasks necessary for us to be completely ready and then calendar backward from presentation day, scheduling each task with an appropriate amount of time for completion. Doing this type of preparation allows us to relax a bit, knowing that we have all the bases covered. It allows us to see the bottlenecks in our process and gives us sufficient time to work them out. It wouldn't be a great presentation without at least one last-minute problem, but that's when the adrenaline kicks in and motivates us to succeed.

Varying our task load is another way to ensure that we remain focused. If we are continually repeating 90-minute cycles of work that require intense concentration, it won't be long before we burn out. But alternating easier tasks with more heavy-duty jobs allows us to remain engaged and helps prevent us from becoming discouraged. We need to continue providing ourselves with challenges, but we don't want the workload to feel endless.

Depending upon your work, you may even be able to alternate two completely different kinds of tasks, such as online research (high intensity) and organizing the supply cabinet (low intensity).

Both activities involve setting and achieving a goal, and both provide tangible results, allowing a feeling of accomplishment upon conclusion. During the low-intensity task, you may even experience a burst of creativity or problem-solving, as your mind wanders freely—bonus.

<u>Adrenaline: Friend or Foe?</u>

Although the hormone adrenaline is often considered the villain in stress scenarios, it's actually highly beneficial to have in specific quantities. Too much adrenaline tends to diminish our ability to focus, but the right amount sharpens our senses. Imagine narrowly avoiding a car accident. Feel the heat as the blood rushes to your head. Your breathing quickens, and your reflexes spring into action, causing you to brake and turn the wheel almost before you realize what's happening. You have adrenaline to thank for facilitating all those actions.

When spurred by an abrupt flash of stress, adrenaline sends a torrent of oxygen-rich red blood cells throughout the body. This boosts your immune system in preparation for immediate danger and triggers the release of painkilling endorphins and dopamine. The brain wants you to focus on one thing: survival. If you have to climb a tree or run through a thicket of thorn bushes to escape an angry bear, the brain wants you to MOVE, not stand around considering the least painful route out of the danger zone. This connects directly with our mid-brain and the instinctual fight-or-flight response designed to keep us safe and alive. Our bodies are firmly hardwired for survival.

This may sound familiar to what was discussed earlier in regards to your brain on stress, but this is your physical reactions to stress.

When we experience a big hit of adrenaline, our body undergoes some drastic changes. That means that our field of vision narrows—we lose nearly all our peripheral vision and can only focus effectively on whatever is directly in front of us. We experience auditory exclusion, meaning that sounds unrelated to the direct threat are filtered out by our brain. We hold our breath or hyperventilate. Many times, these physical changes are necessary to keep us out of harm's way, but what if the threat is not physical, but mental or emotional?

Since our mid-brain can't tell the difference between a real or perceived threat, how do we overcome the physical changes that occur when the adrenaline starts pumping? How can we salvage what might remain of our ability to focus? We have to work on our situational awareness.

Situational awareness is when you attempt to regulate yourself when you understand the source of your arousal or even stress.

Firefighters are a great example of training for situational awareness. Every natural impulse in our bodies tells us to get out when the building is on fire, but they do the opposite. They train constantly to overcome the impulse to run, but every good fireman will tell you that they are never without fear. It's that fear, courtesy of a hormone called noradrenaline, that keeps them alert and on their toes. Noradrenaline provides just the right level of uncertainty to help ensure that we try harder. It puts us just outside of our comfort zone, sharpening our attention and provoking us into optimum performance. Situational awareness takes us off of the cliff's edge and knocks sense back into us.

The effects of too much stress can wreak havoc on our bodies and minds, causing everything from anxiety attacks to hair loss to increased waistlines. Enough light has been shined on the so-called stress epidemic that researchers are finding new and better ways to manage it. Understanding the Yerkes-Dodson Curve can help us shift stress into something beneficial so that we are continually seeking to remain slightly out of our comfort zone in order to encourage ourselves into optimal performance.

Varying our task load—sandwiching easier and harder tasks—serves to keep us engaged and interested and staves off the inevitable burn-out of continuous, intense work. Learning how to tame our situational awareness responses contributes clarity of focus and trains us for future success. With awareness comes the ability to override our natural impulses through use of training (self-discipline) and practice (goal-setting). When we consciously work on managing stress, we'll find it easier to weather things like the Cheetos crisis.

Chapter 6. Singletasking

Sometimes it feels like you're drowning in the amount of work that life gives you. Every day you get a new task or something comes up that you need to cram into your already busy day, and soon enough it can feel overwhelming.

A natural tendency is to start to do everything at once. Dabble a bit here, write a few sentences there. Just multitask, right? Well, actually, that might be just one of the worst things you can do if you're trying to get a job done.

Multitasking is a huge myth.

It's presented as an efficient way to keep up with all the tasks you have to do, but this is just not the case. Everyone thinks they can do it, but there is a big difference between watching television while eating a sandwich and completing two real tasks at once. No one can do it well, even if they think they can, and trying to do it at all will only make you lose focus and end up performing worse at everything.

By multitasking, the only thing that you will achieve is that you will end up continually distracting yourself, because your mind is focused on too many things to process them all equally and efficiently. In fact, according to a study in the *New York Times*, it can take up to 25 minutes to regain focus after being distracted. That's 25 minutes that you will waste trying to find your place and get into the right mindset again. Even if multitasking can seem like the only way forward, the truth is that it will never work.

Attention Residue

Sometimes focusing on work can be difficult, and you find yourself wondering just why it's so hard to stay on track and ignore shiny objects. Luckily, there is an explanation for this. In 2009, Sophie Leroy published a paper that was aptly titled "Why Is it So Hard to Do My Work?" In it, she explained an effect that she called attention residue.

Leroy noted that other researchers had studied the effect of multitasking on performance but that in the modern work environment, once you reached a high enough level, it was more common to find people working on multiple projects sequentially. "Going from one meeting to the next, starting to work on one project and soon after having to transition to another is just part of life in organizations," Leroy explains.

This is essentially the modern version of multitasking—working on projects in short bursts and switching between them, not necessarily doing them all at once. People may not actually be working on multiple tasks at the same time, but it's nearly as bad to keep switching between them in relatively quick succession. For all intents and purposes, this is multitasking.

The problem identified by this research is that you cannot switch seamlessly between tasks without a delay of sorts. When you switch from Task A to Task B, your attention doesn't immediately follow—a residue of your attention remains stuck thinking about the original task. This becomes worse and the residue becomes especially "thick" if your work on Task A was unbounded and of low intensity before you switched, but even if you finish Task A before moving on, your attention remains divided for a while.

Leroy's tests forced people to switch between different tasks in a laboratory setting. In one of these experiments, she started the subjects working on a set of word puzzles. In one of the trials, she would interrupt their work and force them to move on to a new and challenging task—for example, reading resumes and making hypothetical hiring decisions. In other trials, she let the subjects finish the puzzles before giving them the next task.

While the participants were switching between puzzling and hiring, Leroy would play a quick lexical decision game. This was so she could quantify the amount of leftover residue from the first task. The results were clear: "People experiencing attention residue after switching tasks are likely to demonstrate poor performance on that next task," and the more intense the residue, the worse the performance.

This doesn't seem too far of a stretch when you think about it. We've all experienced that frantic moment when we're doing too many things at once and suddenly find ourselves unable to do any at all. How can you concentrate on any task if you keep switching back and forth between two or more different things? You'll likely be stuck simply trying to make sense of everything and organize it so you can understand it. It will only force you to waste time trying to catch up to where you were instead of pushing forward. You'll take one step forward but two steps back each time you try.

Even worse news is presented by a Stanford researcher, Clifford Nass, who examined the work pattern of people who multitask. The researchers split their subjects into two groups: those who regularly do a lot of media multitasking and those who don't. In one experiment, the groups were shown sets of two red rectangles alone or surrounded by two, four, or six blue rectangles. Each configuration was flashed twice, and the participants had to determine whether the two red rectangles in the second frame differed from the first.

It sounds simple enough: just ignore the blue rectangles and see if the red ones change. In fact, it was quite simple, and those who didn't often multitask had no trouble doing this. However, the high multitaskers performed terribly as they were constantly distracted by the irrelevant blue images.

Because they couldn't ignore the images, the researches thought that maybe they were better at storing and organizing information. Maybe they had better memories. But this was proven wrong by the second test. After being shown sequences of alphabetical letters, the high multitaskers also struggled to remember when a letter was making a repeat appearance. And again, the low multitaskers performed better overall. It was as simple as that.

"The low multitaskers did great," Ophir said. "The high multitaskers were doing worse and worse the further they went along because they kept seeing more letters and had difficulty keeping them sorted in their brains."

Multitasking may seem to be the best of both worlds, but when you're in situations where there are multiple sources of information coming from the external world or emerging from memory, you cannot filter out what is irrelevant to your current goal. This failure to filter means that you are slowed down by irrelevant information and will struggle to complete a task without distractions. It is much easier to focus on one thing at once, without letting distractions interfere, than to try doing several things at a time and overload your brain with too much information.

From both of these experiments, it's clear that multitasking isn't really good for anything, and all attempts to do it don't really lead anywhere. By multitasking you are neither able to adequately focus on each new task nor able to ignore any distractions that are hindering your work. There might be certain ways you can multitask 1% more effectively, but the overall lesson is just to avoid it whenever possible.

The answer is in the name of the chapter: singletasking. What does this mean?

To set everything else aside and not check, monitor, email, or even touch anything other than the current task you are working on. It requires singular focus and the purposeful and intentional tuning out of everything else. Switch off your notifications and ditch your phone. If you must be on your computer, keep only one browser tab or program open at a time. A lot of singletasking is about consciously avoiding distractions that seem small and harmless. The biggest culprits? Your electronic devices. Ignore them when possible.

Keep a spotless workspace so your eye doesn't catch something that needs cleaning or adjusting. Ideally, singletasking reduces your environment to a blank room because you shouldn't pay attention to any of it.

Attempt to pay attention to when you are being interrupted or subtly switching between tasks. This is hard to catch at first and will require you to make conscious decisions against your instincts.

Something that will be very hard to resist is to tell yourself that you must act on something immediately and interrupt your task. This is rarely the truth. To combat this urge, set aside a post-it to take notes for ideas that will inevitably spring to mind regarding other tasks. Just jot them down quickly and return to your primary goal. You can address them after your singletasking period is over, and you won't have forgotten anything. It will keep your mind focused on one single task while setting you up for future success.

Flow

Now that we've established why we shouldn't multitask, how should we tackle our workload?

When you don't multitask, you are able to reach a certain momentum and enter into a mode of truly efficient focus. We have all experienced this. It is that moment in the middle of doing a project or assignment that we realize we are actually entirely and wholly focused on completing our task. Time has flown by and yet you are still energized and even obsessed. Distractions are no longer an issue and you find yourself powering through more work than seemed possible, and you're doing it more efficiently than ever before because you are so deeply immersed in your task.

Hungarian psychologist Mihaly Csikszentmihalyi calls this phenomenon a state of "flow," which is what he deems as the most efficient mode of working possible. Csikszentmihalyi describes eight characteristics of flow—what you feel when you're in flow, which also gives you the blueprint to achieve it on a more consistent basis.

Complete concentration on the task. There is no mind wandering or irrelevant thoughts interfering as you work, just complete concentration and focus. When you're in flow, you won't be taking a "break" every five minutes or getting up to do something else when you reach a hurdle. You're powering through the task like there's no tomorrow, and it is taking up all of your attention. Concentration is achieved by removing distractions, being physically ready for such a workload, and immersing yourself into a process without regard for a specific outcome.

Clarity of goals and immediate feedback. Sometimes it can be easy to let ourselves be overwhelmed by the work and let it cloud our end goal. When you're in flow, this is not the case. You have your reward in mind and, with every action you take, success or failure is immediately observed. You know exactly what your purpose is at every second, and this drives you. This immediate feedback helps you push toward your goal in the most direct route by making every decision and action count. Not a second goes by without feeling the feedback of progress. You have the finish line in sight and you are slowly but surely making your way there.

Transformation of time. There is a certain moment when you are so absorbed in your work that you are powering through something that seemed impossible at the beginning. A moment later you look up at the clock and realize several hours have passed while you were in such deep concentration. You work until 2:00 a.m. or you wake up at that time to continue working because you are consumed by these thoughts. Alternatively, you may look up and realize that even though it felt like hours of work, you finished a task in significantly less time than you thought you would. This transformation of time means that you are completely absorbed in your work and have truly reached your flow.

You find the experience intrinsically rewarding. Sometimes when you are doing a task, all you can think about is when you'll finally finish and can never look at it again. But when you're in flow, it is the task itself that you will find rewarding. Sure, you might finish a work project and know that you'll get paid for it. But the act of finishing something that you really tried hard to complete is sometimes reward enough. The worst-case scenario, in a sense, is that you still enjoyed the process, learned something, or derived pleasure from it.

Effortlessness and ease. We have all experienced that moment before a task when we look at the mountain of work that awaits us and feel as if it is an impossible feat. But then we get started and build momentum, and soon enough, we are powering through the work with seemingly no effort at all. This is because momentum is one of the most important things when trying to work through a task. It is considerably easier to keep powering on than to stop for a while and then spend several moments trying to remember where you were and how to continue from there. Start small to feel a sense of victory and then let that feeling carry you through larger and larger tasks.

A balance between challenge and skills. When you are faced with a task that is too difficult, you will feel frustrated or discouraged. When you are faced with a task that is too easy, you will feel bored or underwhelmed. Flow is a state that is just between: the Goldilocks option of the two. It is when your skills perfectly match a task and it is enough of a challenge to keep you excited and stimulated but not overly hard that you just can't make any progress. Overcoming something that you struggled with a little is an amazing feeling—easily finishing a task does nothing for your confidence, and being stopped cold by another task is far too discouraging.

The merging of actions and awareness. There comes a time when you are so immersed in a task that you feel like you don't even need to think about your actions anymore; they just come as naturally as breathing. Your hands move as if through muscle memory, and you instinctively know what to do with each obstacle you come across. You lose the internal monologue, and instead of thinking "now I will place this item in this section," you just do it, because your actions and awareness have completely merged into one. This is what guitarists feel like when they know a song extremely well—their fingers just move without conscious thought.

Finally, there is a feeling of control over the task. This isn't to be confused with dominance over the task or a feeling of absolute authority. This is more the kind of control where you have no worries or insecurities interfering with your progress and you are fully aware of every action or decision you make and know that you are constantly getting closer to your end goal. You can foresee everything that will happen and what exactly will be needed.

Obviously, flow is the end result of a complete and thorough focus on a task. How do you get into the realm of flow? By enjoying yourself, stopping any multitasking, finding a balance between challenge and ease, and finding a way to completely immerse yourself in your work.

It is the same feeling as being "in the zone" or being "on fire." It is all the same principle. This is something that every athlete knows. Whether they are a swimmer or tennis player, they all reach a stage of feeling completely and utterly focused on their sport. Every action is completely linked to trying to win or succeed, and there are no distractions and definitely no multitasking to slow them down. It should be clear that flow can't necessarily be summoned at will, but you can aspire to fulfill individual characteristics and be better focused as a result.

Deep Work

Similar to the idea of flow, and another alternative to multitasking, is Cal Newport's concept of "deep work." According to Newport, deep work is classified as "professional activities performed in a state of distraction-free concentration that push your cognitive capabilities to their limits." So basically, it is a state of focus that is taking up all of your concentration, which happens to ensure that you become necessarily bored, which will pay dividends.

Despite that, deep work doesn't have to be tedious. In fact, it often culminates in creative, thought-provoking realizations that you would have never reached otherwise. What are the principles of deep work to integrate into your life?

The first tactic is to *work deeply*. It can take great patience, practice, and perseverance to get to the point where you can integrate long stretches of deep work into your schedule. It's so easy to get distracted by even the littlest things: a phone call, an email, something good on television, or even the fridge. The hardest part of a job is often just sitting down to get it done. Look at your schedule and truly block out a period of time where you are essentially in a windowless room without your phone. It sounds like a long time, but that's exactly the point—your mind will wander, and it's this wandering that pays huge dividends.

Newport created an equation to explain the intensity required of deep work and compared it to students who pulled all-nighters in college.

Work accomplished = (time spent) × (intensity)

When you work at a high level with dynamic and intense intervals that increase over time, you will produce a desirable outcome. Get in the zone for at least 90 minutes and build up to periods that last anywhere from two to four hours or more. By doing this, you will get the best quality and quantity of work actually accomplished.

The second of Newport's tactics is to get into the habit of protecting your time. You cannot immediately start doing long hours of deep work every day if you are not used to it. You just won't be able to stick with it. Additionally, it's not always realistic to be able to block off three hours of time away from everyone else in the world. Therefore, the best way to integrate deep work into your life is to become great at protecting your time.

You can do this by scheduling tactics into your workflow like tallies, where you keep a tally of the hours you spend working or when you reach important milestones such as pages read or words written. As well as tallies, you could also try scheduling deep work hours well in advance on a calendar, perhaps two or even four weeks in advance to make sure you have it cemented in your plans. Make these hours set in stone in such a way that everything and everyone else has to work around these non-negotiables. Another tactic is to grow more comfortable with saying no to people by differentiating if you are doing it out of some obligation or guilt versus actually wanting to do it.

Finally, keep your priorities in mind. Are you unable to protect your time because you would rather save people's feelings and highly inconvenience yourself? This is a symptom of people-pleasing and fear of judgment. Thus, find an easy scapegoat such as your schedule or life circumstances.

Protect your time and allow yourself to build up to blocks of deep work more frequently and organically. You will accustom your body and mind to this new method of working deeply and produce overall better results. A long-distance runner will not start out by running 10 miles after never having done it before. You will simply not be able to do it efficiently or easily. Instead, by slowly adding hours and miles, lengthening the time of running and the intensity of the run, you will be able to gradually increase your skill and you will be more used to going farther distances.

In the same way, by protecting your time, keeping tallies, and slowly increasing the hours of deep work that you do, you will be able to accustom yourself to working for longer at higher intensities and thus accomplish more work. Stamina is not optional, and of course this helps your focus in general.

Overall, work is hard but multitasking is not the answer. Instead, aim to invest in the concepts of flow and deep work in order to maximize your efficiency. To succeed in your tasks, you need to learn to focus on one thing at once and deeply submerge yourself in it so that you can focus all your energy into completing it and doing the best job that you possibly can.

Chapter 7. Productivity

Productivity is something we always want to improve. That's probably the end goal you want in the quest for improving your focus. No matter who we are or how hard we work, there is always something we could be doing to take advantage of the time we do have and fit as many things in as possible. When you're distracted or can't focus on a task, your productivity levels are considerably decreased because you're not working as efficiently as you could be.

What's important is to learn to focus on your task and make sure you are doing all you can to be as productive as possible. Sometimes this can seem impossible, or you may feel that you have to make really big changes and restrictions in order to be as productive as you can.

Fortunately, you don't have to make big changes. There are plenty of little things you can do to boost your productivity and have you feeling as if your days are never wasted.

Track Everything

This can seem tedious but it's been proven to be one of the best motivators there are. When researchers have studied the effects of a given activity, they found that candidates are more likely to improve and do more when they are asked to track a specific outcome. For example, people have been assigned to wear pedometers to measure how far they walk each day. When faced with a means of tracking their actual walking progress, people walked at least one extra mile every day on average and improved their overall activity levels by 27%.

It's a simple method. The fact is, most of the time, we're all in denial about something or another. When you are asked to track something and write down or pay attention to a specific number, you will be more motivated to improve it because you are faced with the actual truth. You will feel shame or encouragement, both of which are motivating. The act of committing to something and being held accountable for it, and knowing that there is no way to get around a solid figure, will make your progress increase dramatically. Tracking progress honestly doesn't allow you to lie and sometimes the truth can be a dramatic wake-up call.

So as the section title instructs, track *everything*.

Start by tracking your time. Measure *exactly* how you are spending every moment of the day, with no cheating or rounding of the numbers. If you spend an hour watching a movie, write it down. If you spend an hour playing with your cat, write it down. If you spend time getting sucked down the rabbit hole of Wikipedia, write it down. Use increments of 15 minutes.

The purpose is that at the end of every day you will look back at the tasks you have done that day and know how productive you were. You'll see how much time you actually spend on what you want versus what you think you are doing. You will undoubtedly see you have been wasting hours of time each day you thought you were being "busy" or "productive." How many 15-minute increments could you have avoided or were truly wasteful?

You'll still feel an urge to waste time with some silly activity or procrastinate for several hours. But because you'll have to write it down and quantify exactly how many hours you do waste, you'll just find yourself not wanting to do that to yourself. This what-gets-measured-gets-improved effect means that you will want to start spending more time on highly productive or valuable activities just so you feel great at the end of the day and don't have to look at what you could have done better.

By creating an accountability chart to measure and list how productive you were and what tasks you actually accomplished in a day, you will be able to visually see how successful you have been. And once you do that, you'll also be able to visually see how much you improve every day just because of this one trick.

If it's not worth measuring, then the truth is that it's not worth doing because of the lack of accountability. What else can you measure besides time?

Small Victories

So you're having an amazing day. You finished everything on time at work and even did a little bit extra, something that your boss is sure to notice. You got a free muffin with your coffee and it's been the perfect temperature all day, sunny but with just a little wind so that it's not too hot. You've never felt better. But then, all of a sudden, you lose an important file or you've forgotten about an important meeting and your good mood could not have fled faster, despite the perfect day you've just had.

It's hard to admit it, but we are all a bunch of negative people. No, really. Science says so. Research proves that your brain has a negativity bias. It is simply built with a greater sensitivity to unpleasant news and the bias is so automatic that it can be easily detected at the earliest stage of the brain's information processing.

John Cacioppo, Ph.D., then at Ohio State University, now at the University of Chicago, conducted some studies to prove this. He showed people several images that are known to have specific feelings attached. For example, a Ferrari or a pizza to prompt positive feelings, a mutilated face or a dead cat to prompt negative feelings, and a plate or a hair dryer for neutral feelings. As he did this, he recorded the electrical activity in the brain's cerebral cortex, which reflects the magnitude of information processing taking place.

Cacioppo demonstrated that the brain has a significantly more intense reaction to stimuli that it deems negative than those that it deems positive. The surge in electrical activity is far greater. This means that our attitudes are more heavily influenced by downbeat news than good news—and so are our reactions.

Before we continue down this negative road, it's important to point out that our capacity to weigh the negatives so heavily most likely evolved for a good reason. Because of our significant reaction to negative stimuli, we would probably be more prone to avoid danger. From the dawn of time, our entire survival depended upon keeping out of danger and dodging predators. Thus, the brain developed a way that would make it impossible for us to not notice danger and, hopefully, respond to it.

So what does this mean for you? Are you forever doomed to be in a perpetually negative state because of this negativity bias?

Luckily, this is not the case, and there are many things you can do to balance out this negativity bias, especially when it comes to your productivity.

Following on from the last point of tracking time, it is also important to track your victories and accomplishments, *especially* the small ones. When you track the tiny accomplishments, you can address the bias and you will be giving yourself tiny dopamine spikes throughout the day at every accomplishment. Simply making a list and crossing things off will do, and you will feel a small sense of achievement every time you finish even the smallest activity.

Keep a daily accomplishment list or a to-do list with as many tiny goals as you can so that you can keep track of every positive thing that you do. By tracking your small victories, you are basically keeping up your positivity and thus your motivation, allowing you to stay focused because of your constant achievements and the positivity that this will bring to your working attitude. With so many victories, no matter how small they are, you will be continuously inspired to keep working hard and keep earning as many victories as you can.

Newton's First Law of Momentum

This one might seem a stretch at first glance, but we can say there is sufficient *science* involved.

Let's set the scene. You have a big task due and you probably should have started a lot earlier. You know what has to be done, but every time you try to start, you hit a roadblock or something gets in the way and you've found yourself making no progress. Sound familiar? Luckily, our good friend and famed physicist Isaac Newton can help us out.

Newton's First Law of Motion:
"An object at rest stays at rest and an object in motion stays in motion."

Where is this going? To boost your productivity and stop falling into these slumps of unproductiveness, get in motion and stay in motion. This begins from the moment you wake up. The first few hours of your day often determine how the rest of it will go, so get up on the right side of bed and start your productivity as soon as you can. Set the tone for the day you want and create motion for yourself as soon as possible. Otherwise, it's too possible to watch videos and read entertainment news for hours—because that's the tone you've set for the day.

Here are a few things you can do to have the best type of morning for productivity and momentum.

Plan everything. There is no use waking up, ready for a productive day, and then spending 30 minutes looking for a shirt that has mysteriously gone missing or even trying to put your day's tasks into order. Plan everything the night before so you can exercise as little brainpower in the morning as possible.

Get your outfit ready, your breakfast ready, everything you need to take to work or school ready. Write down your focus or work objectives the night before and have a clear idea of exactly what you will be doing. The most productive morning is one where you wake up and are instantly able to take action instead of staying still and thinking.

Don't snooze your alarm clock. It's tempting, so very tempting. But you *know* five more minutes can so easily turn into 30 and so easily mean that you are late for something important. Even if you have a day off, plan to wake up at a reasonable hour. It might seem like a small thing, but think of the morning hours wasted without an alarm. You're also committing to starting your day with an act of self-discipline and focus.

Don't start with email. This seems a bit odd at first glance. Sometimes the very first thing you do to start your morning is checking your email to see if anyone wants anything from you. More often than not, the answer is yes; people always want something from you and they want it yesterday. Well, that's the opposite of creating focus for yourself, isn't it? Understand your own priorities first and *then* start on the emails.

Emails are a to-do list that other people have made for you. We don't realize this. But if something is important or urgent enough, people will make an effort to contact you in other ways. And if it's not that important, eventually a non-response to an email will fade into irrelevancy. In other words, feel free to actually *be* worse with email because others will compensate for it and the world will not fall apart.

Once you've done what you need to do for yourself, then you can start on what other people need from you and treat email as crossing something off your list.

Start with the little things. It's hard to get motivated and keep momentum when the first piece of work you do is one that will take hours and can often not show any significant feedback or progress. Instead, start with the small tasks that need to be done—ones you can do quickly so that you can immediately make visible progress. This way, you get the ball rolling as soon as you can and you can keep up your motivation as you head for bigger and more challenging tasks. It's easy to get started when you can ease into warming up your brain, so to speak.

Finally, aim to do as much as you can before noon. This could be different for other people, but when noon hits, I immediately think I'm over the halfway point of my day, even if this is not the case. It's a massive psychological barrier. Noon means lunch is near, and then that inevitable period of time where you break your focus and must scramble to find your place afterwards. And of course, it's tough to recapture the mood. By breaking momentum, you may never find it again that day, so do as much as you can in the morning hours when you're already in the zone before you have to take a break in the afternoon. Make it a competition—against yourself.

It's hard enough to get through your tasks of the day without being focused and in the right mindset. However, if you follow the wise words of Isaac Newton, you'll find that creating motion to begin your day means that you will be less likely to stop or slow down, and the work will be done before you know it.

Implementation Intention

Your mindset is the most important part of your productivity. If you're not feeling productive or you can't get into the zone, you just won't produce the results that you want. One way to fix this is to reframe your goals and your mindsets. *Implementation intention* is a system for you to do this, where you reframe your goals as "if-then" statements.

Let's break that down. You need to set your goals up in a way that will assist you in overcoming hurdles and striving for success. You need to think of matters in the following way: *if* this happens, *then* I will do this. The *if* part is a situation, and the *then* part is your response. Decide on something that you want or need to accomplish. Then tie that to a condition. It's an effective way to overcome any obstacles and reach your goals.

The concept of implementation intentions, introduced by Peter Gollwitzer, a professor of psychology at New York University, has been around since 1999. Studies have found this technique to cause an increase in progress toward goals over a whopping 7.7 times greater. The purpose is for you to anticipate a situation and then your behavior in response, a response that is aimed toward a specific goal.

Here are a few examples.

First, have a goal in mind. If you are trying to boost your productivity, you might want your goal to be reducing phone use. After you set this goal, your thinking should shift to *"if* I am doing work at my desk, *then* I will turn off my phone. This way you set up a situation and your response to it is one that will help you reach your goal. If you get into a mindset for this example where you can only use your phone when not at your desk, eventually you will reach a point where it's not worth leaving your desk just to use your phone and instead you will keep working.

Another example might be that you want to exercise more so you can start your day off with some energy. In this case, you might think "*if* I wake up at 7:00 a.m., *then* I will go to the gym." You can try this method with any other scenario as long as it features an if-then statement and is targeted at you reaching a particular goal. You are taking two independent acts and pairing them together in a way that chains them together. Instead of the instinct to throw one punch in defense, the instinct becomes throwing two punches in quick succession.

Why does this work? The big reason is because you eliminate choice. When there are too many options on how to proceed, a lot of the time these only act as obstacles in the way of our goals. Implementation intentions remove choices and focus on situations that you will commonly face, forcing you down a path that you know is the best course of action and one that will ultimately lead to one of your goals.

It also works because it automates responses. If you've already decided exactly what you're going to do, then everything becomes significantly easier. This can be applied to everything in life; having a plan even for the smallest things can make everything easier. If you think of the frustration when you're stuck in line behind someone who takes 30 minutes to order a simple coffee, you will understand that decisiveness is the number one ally you can have.

When you've got a plan or decision for something you know will happen, you won't forget to act or miss an opportunity that will benefit you, nor will you waste time deliberating. You will be less swayed in the heat of the moment by those attractive short-term benefits and instead choose the long-term benefits almost automatically.

Finally, this method also conserves willpower. Sticking to a decision drains a lot of willpower, even if we know it is the right thing to do. This method bypasses the fatigue of self-control and decision-making because you already know exactly what you should and will do, and you know that by doing it, you will be one step closer to your goals.

Productivity is something that you need to constantly work on. Being productive can be as simple as deciding to do so and as discussed above; you only need to make a few small changes in order to receive big rewards. It's all about your attitude and mindset, so track your valuable time, celebrate the small victories, keep yourself moving, and implement your intentions. It is these little changes that will result in the most productive days overall.

Chapter 8. Tactics

This chapter is for the small things that can make a big difference in your focus. Some of them you might expect on some level, but others might be completely counter to your intuition, as no doubt some concepts in this book already have been.

Consume Less Media

This isn't a point about being less informed or less worldly, so to speak. Rather, it's to point out that most of what makes the news these days is negative to some degree. There's a reason the slogan, "If it bleeds, it leads" is used to describe the news. Studies have quoted the ratio of positive news (couple reunites after 20 years apart) to negative news (burglary in local jewelry store) at 17:1—this must have a cumulative effect.

Even if you don't want to hear a particularly negative story, it may find its way to your ears and eyes. We've talked about how stress has quite an effect on your focus because of how it puts your body into a mode where focus is biologically destroyed. Being negative invites stress and anxiety, which themselves are force multipliers. They cause you to doubt yourself, think pessimistically, and sour your ability to focus.

How do you feel after watching a news segment on the rising murder rate or a genocide somewhere in the world? Perhaps a documentary on poverty?

Skipping the news and consuming positive information instead of negative information can help you with your focus. Your mood is a force multiplier, so you may as well attempt to keep it as positive as possible and keep the stress hormones away. It all boils down to the simple question of whether you can get more done if you've just eaten ice cream or if you are on the verge of tearing your hair out. Stay Zen by avoiding negative news, negative people, and negativity in general. It makes you happier and keeps you more able to focus.

Batching

Henry Ford, founder of Ford Motor Company, got a lot of things right about cars.

He had a few competitors back in the day, but a primary reason those names are essentially lost in time is because he was also the creator of the *factory assembly line*. On a factory assembly line, workers focus on one task at a time.

This streamlines a process and makes it far more efficient than having a single worker see a project through from start to finish, switching between multiple tasks. It allows workers to specialize and perfect their task, which cuts down on errors and makes troubleshooting far easier. Workers didn't have to do more thinking than was necessary for the task at hand. For Ford, this made his automobile production efficiency and output shoot through the roof and dominate his market.

That, in essence, is what *batching* can do for you.

Batching is when you group similar tasks together to complete them all at once. Ford's assembly line was essentially 100% batching because his workers only performed one task incredibly efficiently.

Let's take a common example we can all relate to—checking email.

If you have any sort of online presence or job, you probably have a steady stream of emails trickling (or gushing) into your inbox every hour. Constantly checking your email is an extremely inefficient use of time. It interrupts other tasks and scatters your focus whenever you receive a new email. Many of us drop what we're doing to take care of something from an email. Then we have to start the original task over again because our flow and momentum has been interrupted.

Batching emails will considerably improve your productivity. An example of this would be to only check your emails at the top of every two hours and purposely ignore or block your inbox notifications. At first it might be difficult, but limiting how often you check email in this way allows you to focus on your tasks without constantly being distracted and having to re-acclimatize yourself.

Perhaps more importantly, it teaches the lesson that saying no to some tasks is just as important as saying yes to the correct ones. Batching teaches the art of purposeful, deliberate ignorance so you can focus on other tasks.

Switching from task to task is a large mental burden because you are essentially stopping and starting from zero numerous times throughout the day. It takes a lot of energy to switch from task to task, and there are usually a few wasted minutes just regaining your bearings and figuring out the status of the task you were working on. Of course, these kinds of interruptions only lead to achieving just a portion of what you can and want to.

In the example of checking email, batching allows you to stay in a mindset of reading and composing email with all its associated skills, tasks, and reminders. Email is a distinctly different mindset and way of thinking than designing a new graphic for an advertising campaign. Staying in the same mindset pays huge dividends.

Batching allows you to save your mental energy for the tasks themselves and not waste your energy on the process of switching back and forth between them.

What else can you batch? You can schedule all your meetings in one afternoon so you will have a free, uninterrupted morning to work. You can plan to do everything that requires computer access in the morning and even batch parts of tasks such as the parts that require you to make phone calls.

You can also batch your distractions. This isn't to distract and amuse yourself more efficiently; it's to make sure that you are conserving your energy and allowing your focused time to be exactly that—focused.

How can you batch distractions? For example, if you're burned out on a particular task, you might want to take a little social media break. By all means, take it! However, allot just a bit more time to check *all* of your accounts: ESPN, Refinery29, and whatever other distractions you occupy yourself with. Grab a new cup of coffee, take a brisk walk around the office, and say hello to your neighbor.

Get it all out of your system so that when you're back to work, you can have a solid and fixed block of time in which to focus. After all, if there is nothing new on your Facebook page, you will probably feel less compelled to check it. Once you knock yourself out doing all these distracting activities within the allotted time, you can switch to productive work for the rest of your hour.

The more you divide your attention among different activities, the less productive you'll be. However, if you begin doing something similar to the previous activity; you'll find it's much easier to get going because your mind is already geared toward doing a certain kind of task. Do all the similar tasks together, one after the other, and then move on to the next batch of similar or related activities. Effective batching can skyrocket your productivity no matter the context.

"Don't-Do" List

Everyone knows the value of the to-do list—no doubt you've stumbled across tips elsewhere about using a to-do list to increase productivity.

But everyone inherently *kind of* knows what they should be doing and when they need to do it by. The act of writing it down just helps remind them, and makes people more likely to take care of their obligations.

However, not everyone knows what they *shouldn't* be doing—what they should be avoiding, common ways of procrastinating, and distractions that masquerade as priorities. Along with your to-do list, it's equally important to make a *don't-do list*. Each day, we're faced with choosing tasks that will create the biggest impact for us, and there are many hidden obstacles.

Again, we all know the obvious evils to avoid when trying to upgrade productivity: social media, goofing around on the Internet, watching *The Bachelorette* while trying to work, and learning to play the flute while reading.

It can be difficult to distinguish between real tasks and useless tasks, and it will require some hard thought on your part. You need to fill your don't-do list with tasks that will sneakily steal your time and undermine your goals. These are tasks that are insignificant or a poor use of your time, tasks that don't help your bottom line, and tasks that have a serious case of diminishing returns the more you work on them.

If you continuously devote and waste your time on these tasks, your real priorities and goals will be left untouched. Here's what you should put on your *don't*-do list.

First, include tasks that are priorities, but which you can't do anything about at present because of external circumstances.

These are tasks that are important in one or many ways, but are waiting for feedback from others, or for underlying tasks to be completed first. Put these on your don't-do list because there is literally nothing you can do about them!

Don't spend your mental energy thinking about them. They'll still be there when you hear back from those other people. Just note that you are waiting to hear back from someone else and note the date on which you need to follow-up if you haven't heard back. Then, push these out of your mind because they're on someone else's to-do list, not yours. You can also temporarily push things off your plate by clarifying and asking questions of other people. This puts the ball in their court to act, and you can take that time to catch up on other matters.

Second, include tasks that don't add value as far as your projects are concerned.

There are many small items that don't add to your bottom line, and often these are trivial things—busy work. Can you delegate these, assign them to someone else, or even outsource them? Do they really require your time? In other words, are they *worth* your time? And will anyone but you notice the difference if you delegate the task to someone else? By taking on the task yourself, are you getting stuck in the weeds of perfectionism? You should spend your time on big tasks that move entire projects forward and not myopic, trivial tasks. Often these are useless tasks disguised as important ones, such as selecting the paint color for the bike shed in the parking lot of the nuclear power plant you are building.

Third, include tasks that are current and ongoing but will not benefit from additional work or attention paid to them.

These tasks suffer from diminishing returns. These tasks are just a waste of energy because while they can still stand to improve (and is there anything that can't?), and the amount of likely improvement will either not make a difference in the overall outcome or success or will take a disproportionate amount of time and effort without making a significant dent.

For all intents and purposes, these tasks should be considered *done*. Don't waste your time on them, and don't fall into the trap of considering them a priority. Once you finish everything else on your plate, you can then evaluate how much time you want to devote to polishing something.

If the task is at 90% of the quality you need it to be, it's time to look around at what else needs your attention to bring it from 0% to 90%. In other words, it's far more helpful to have three tasks completed at 80% quality versus one task at 100% quality.

When you consciously avoid the items on your don't-do list, you keep yourself focused and streamlined. You don't waste energy or time, and your daily output will increase dramatically.

Why read a menu with food items that are unavailable? It's pointless and wastes your mental bandwidth. By preventing your energy level from being dissipated by those things that suck up your time and attention, a don't-do list enables you to focus on what matters.

This can have a very dramatic and positive impact on your daily routine. The fewer things that tug on your mind, the better—the kind of stress and anxiety they create only hampers or kills productivity. A don't-do list will free your mind from the burden of having too many things in the air because it eliminates most of those things! You can focus on the balls that are still in flight and steadily knock each one out.

ABCDE

A straightforward to-do list can be just as unproductive as having nothing at all. It can make you spin your wheels, create anxiety, and cause more confusion than it should.

After finishing a task, you can very easily slip into the danger zone that arises when you attempt to select your next task, creating a loss of focus. Just think about the uptick in efficiency you would create if you had to make 100 phone calls and you kept the phone to your ear between calls. Once you put the phone down, you'll inevitably find a reason to wander off before the next call.

This occurs if you only list every task you need to complete without priority or organization. If you've got a to-do list that simply lists 10 tasks, how do you even know where to start? Do you start from the top and work your way down to the bottom?

You can spend 10 minutes trying to make sense of your task landscape every time you glance at it, or you can use categories to effectively milk the most from your list. A list for a list's sake doesn't accomplish everything you need it to in an efficient way; it only ensures you don't forget tasks. Break your list into categories that will let you know exactly how to spend each minute of your day.

It's called the ABCDE priority list.

This method involves filtering your list in terms of preset priorities and consequences. This allows you to catalog your time, focus on the immediate priorities, and make sure nothing slips through the cracks.

Just as importantly, it will also let you know what you *don't* need to worry about, so you can decrease your mental strain and focus on one thing at a time.

The ABCDE priority list has five categories.

"A" = Very Important

An "A" task means the item is very important and needs to be done immediately. It is your first priority. You can't wait on others for this, and you're the only one that action depends on.

You *must* take care of it today, and there are serious negative consequences if you fail to do so. It's a strict deadline that overrides any of the other tactics in this book—you simply need to get this done first or second.

Regardless of the stakes, there will be harm if you don't complete this "A" task. That's the easiest way to tell whether an item is truly very important or is a lower-priority item. If your life will be negatively affected from failure to complete something that day, it belongs in the "A" category. This includes your own internal deadlines.

Urgency level: that hour or day.

Teacher example: writing a test that you will give later that day.

Of note, when you consider your "A" tasks, you should keep the Pareto Principle in mind. The Pareto Principle forces you to examine your workflow and determine the main activities that move the needle—what 20% of actions are driving 80% of the results? This phenomenon occurs almost everywhere there are tasks that compete for attention. Some of them truly matter, while others are decorative or even optional. So what are the high-leverage activities you can focus on and prioritize in this category?

When you force yourself to examine your tasks, you might find that most of them are actually time-wasters (the rest of the 80% of the work) in disguise.

"B" = Important

In the "B" section of your priority list, you should include items that you *should* do that day. Compare these with "A" items. "A" items are the things you *must* do. If you don't do them, there will be large negative consequences.

"B" tasks don't create consequences of that magnitude, which is how you differentiate "A" from "B" tasks. The consequences of not completing an "A" task might be catastrophic and unredeemable, whereas the consequences of not completing a "B" task might be fixable and minor in the long run.

It may be worth skipping over a "B" task solely to complete an "A" task. This fallout will be worth it for the greater good of the "A" task. Incidentally, this is what separates "B" items from the rest of the hierarchy. There are still negative consequences with the failure to complete a "B" task, but there are none for "C," "D," and "E" tasks.

Following up with others and making sure things are on track to be completed or replied to are also "B" tasks.

Urgency level: after "A" tasks, whether at the end of the day or the next day.

Teacher example: give homework for that night and prepare a lecture for the next day.

"C" = Nice to Do

In any priority list, there are always optional items you keep around just to make sure that you don't forget about them. Many people tend to confuse these items with the necessary tasks for the day, which makes this category all the more important.

As the category title says, these are tasks that would be *nice to do*. They aren't necessary for the day, and there is nothing riding on their completion. They're extra and exist purely if you want to work ahead or start a new initiative.

They might bring secondary value to the other tasks you have, and they might position you for better opportunities in the future. "C" tasks aren't about the present; they are about thinking ahead and working for the future. Having a good handle on "C" tasks is what will truly double your output. We all know our "A" and "B" tasks, but we rarely catalog what we should do with our extra time (besides relax).

For example, networking, sending cold emails, meeting with new potential business partners, and updating your resume are all "C" tasks. So are tasks that you've put off for longer periods of time, like chores and taxes. They are future-facing. There aren't any negative consequences if you don't do these things, just lost opportunities.

Urgency level: at the end of the day or whenever there is time during the week.

Teacher example: work on your curriculum for the next semester.

"D" = Delegate

These are the tasks you can delegate to coworkers and friends or outsource completely.

Keep in mind that there is a big difference between delegation and outsourcing. Delegation means there are people working under you or you have specialized divisions at your work that you can assign work to. Outsourcing, on the other hand, actually involves virtual assistants doing your job.

"D" tasks are things that you can assign to someone else. Often, they are tasks that *should* be taken care of by others and that you should let go of and trust someone else to do. "D" tasks are often a waste of your time to do yourself. They can probably be done by somebody else at the same level of quality.

When you're faced with a "D" task, you must ask yourself if you would pay X amount of money to be rid of it and not have to worry about it. Is your time worth more than the cost of having someone else do the task? If you're not in a position to delegate or outsource these tasks, you might have to move them up in priority to just behind the "A" and "B" tasks.

They need to be done, but not necessarily by you.

Teacher example: you can outsource or delegate decorating the classroom to the students themselves.

"E" = Eliminate

These are tasks that you should forget and take off your plate completely. This concept is similar to the don't-do list.

You can eliminate more tasks than you think with zero negative consequences. In many cases, these tasks just weigh on your mind and may overwhelm you with a false sense of urgency and emotional stress. Additionally, when they occupy space on your to-do list, you are unable to escape the mental strain associated with thinking about them.

What should you eliminate? Tasks that suffer from diminishing returns, that are already delegated, that are waiting for input from others, and that simply aren't necessary to your goals within the next month or two. File future aspirations away in a separate folder and keep them out of your daily field of vision.

Teacher example: detailed reports on each child's grasp of physical education.

The ABCDE priority list is a method of making your life more focused and more capable of focusing.

Just Say "Don't"

Learning how to say no to temptation and distraction is one of the most useful skills you can develop. You don't focus when you continually say yes to the chatter around you and especially the people around you.

Saying no to unnecessary commitments can give you the time you need to re-calibrate yourself and seize control of your own schedule. Many people struggle with this, and in fact, there is a more optimal way of saying no to people and things other than simply having to dig deep into your reserve of willpower. A study published in the *Journal of Consumer Research* found that a simple semantic difference made saying no exponentially easier.

The study used two groups of subjects, and each group was faced with a temptation. The first group was told to repeat that they *can't* partake in the temptation, and the second group was told to repeat that they *don't* partake in the temptation. For instance, if the temptation was alcohol, the first group would say, "I *can't* drink right now" while the second group would say, "I *don't* drink."

As each subject left the study, they were offered a choice of a food item; one healthy and one unhealthy. What ended up happening was that the subjects in the first group (can't) chose the unhealthy food item 61% of the time while the subjects in the second group (don't) chose the unhealthy food item only 36% of the time. This highly suggests that switching one word in how people refused a temptation made it extremely easier to say no to subsequent temptations.

Why was this?

The words you choose to frame your state of mind convey one of two things. If you tend to use the word *can't*, then you are reminding yourself of something you must actively resist. *Can't* is to say that you would but that you are unable to at the moment due to some reason, most likely because you are imposing a restriction on yourself. If you think about it, we use *can't* when we exercise willpower and discipline.

However, when you use *don't*, you are giving yourself power in the situation. You are subconsciously saying that you have already made a decision so there is nothing you need to exercise self-discipline over. *Don't* means there is no more room for discussion; it imposes a rule you have set yourself. If you ask someone to eat an unhealthy meal with you, what is your response to (1) "I can't today because I'm on a diet" versus (2) "I don't eat unhealthy." The latter is far more definite than the other and invites little to no debate. This is the same process that occurs subconsciously.

These are two words that may seem interchangeable, but they have a very different psychological impact that will result in very different actions and focus.

Start with one tactic at a time and implement it slowly. This is how behavioral change will turn into habit and remain sustainable.

Chapter 9. Odds and Ends

After the last chapter, we've established that focus is required for any real attempt at productive work. We also know that focus is hard to achieve even at the best of times because so many of life's distractions are just at our fingertips. Fortunately, there are plenty of scientifically proven tips that can help you find and maintain your focus. Some of these may be a little odd, but they all work and will help you concentrate on whatever task needs to be done.

<u>Chewing Gum</u>

The first tip is perhaps the strangest of the lot and may be also the simplest: chewing gum. How can something as easy as chewing gum help you improve your focus? Well, research done by the *British Journal of Psychology* shows that chewing gum increases the oxygen flow to certain parts of your brain that are responsible for your attention span—the prefrontal cortex, which resides over what are generally known as *executive functions*. This extra oxygen means that you will be more alert and your reflexes will improve as well.

Seems too good to be true? Well, there's more. The increased blood flow also improves your long-term memory so that you are able to store and recall more information. This is very helpful when you are trying to study or learn material for work or if you need to remember specific protocols at work. Gum also injects a little bit of insulin into your blood. This little bit of insulin gives you an added energy boost, reinvigorating your brain and motivating you to get out of that slump that you may find yourself in.

So gum is actually a really effective booster of mental performance. Best of all, unlike many other mental performance enhancers, gum itself is responsible for all sorts of benefits without any side effects. The latest investigation into gum is from a team of psychologists at St. Lawrence University. They conducted an experiment to see the effect of gum on the brain and whether it actually did help to improve performance.

The experiment went like this: 159 students were presented with a number of very demanding cognitive tasks such as repeating random numbers backward and trying to solve challenging logic puzzles. Half of the subjects chewed gum (sugar-free and sugar-added) while the other half didn't chew anything.

Here's where things got interesting. The subjects who were randomly assigned to chew gum significantly outperformed the others in five out of six of the tests. The only exception was in the sixth test, which was in verbal fluency, where subjects needed to name as many words as possible from a given category, such as "animals." The gum's sugar content had no effect on the performance.

Even though it seems hard to believe, gum might just be the answer to your struggling work cycle. It's a cheap and easy method to try to give you the added push to get you sucked back into your work. If you're not a gum fan, you can still use this research to help you. Gum increases attention span because it increases oxygen flow to the brain. You can replicate this by taking short exercise breaks through your day—even just five minutes to tackle some stairs and you will be more alert. If you can't exercise, sometimes taking a break to breathe very deeply for a moment or two can be more than helpful.

It improves not only your attention span, but also your memory, which is perfect to help you get out of any work slumps that you may be having. That's not to say that you'll immediately be able to finish that mountain of work you've been avoiding for far too long, but gum may just be a quick way to help get you back on track and focused once more.

Quiet

The next tip is silence. This one is a little bit more believable at first glance, but not necessarily for the reasons you might think. Because we are so prone to distraction, even the slightest noise can often pull us out of our concentrated state and lead us away from our work. The expression "I can't hear myself think" is entirely true. When we are surrounded by noise, we cannot successfully go about our regular thought processes because of how noise can distract us.

Research into the effect of noise on our brains shows that there is even a deeper reason why we cannot work with it.

Ambient noise of any kind, like cars honking or kids screaming, can stimulate the release of the stress hormone, cortisol. Mark A.W. Andrews, former director of the Lake Erie College of Osteopathic Medicine at Seton Hill University in Pennsylvania, has studied this in depth. He told *Scientific American* that too much cortisol could impair function and hinder focus. Cortisol, of course, is the body's stress hormone that puts someone into fight-or-flight mode. Worse yet, the more we are exposed to ambient noise, the worse our body's response will be.

This means that every time you are in the middle of working and any noise disrupts you, you will feel more stressed and thus distracted from your work. Over time, this will mean that even the slightest noise will make you completely unable to work.

So what's the solution? Silence, of course. Knowing that you need to keep all noise to a minimum means that you should try and design your workspace so that you can block out any distracting noise and keep it as quiet as you can.

There is noise everywhere, and this can be difficult, but reducing it as much as you can will significantly help your concentration levels. This includes little things such as the clock that's ticking on your office wall. It may seem small and you might not even notice it, but you will be considerably calmer without it there.

If you can't redesign your workspace, then perhaps you can use music to your advantage. If you can get simple and relaxing music playing in the background, covering up or softening any harsh noises, then that can also work just as well as reducing noise all together. Alternatively, some ambient noise can be relaxing. If you're lucky enough to work in a place where the only ambient sound is that of nature, the wind blowing or the ocean, maybe reducing it is not the way to go. For others, complete silence makes them tense and stressed. Play around and see what works best for you.

Meditation

The third tip for stronger focus is meditation. Many people are put off by the mention of mediation because they immediately imagine sitting cross-legged on the ground, hands places on knees, and humming loudly. However, meditation comes in many forms and its main objective is to focus your mind and stretch your self-awareness, something that can be beyond useful especially when you're trying to be more focused on your work.

A recent paper in *Psychological Science* tried to identify the brain functions that meditating actually enhances. This study shows that performing intensive meditation not only helps focus your attention, but also allows you to sustain it—even during the most boring of tasks.

The study was led by Katherine MacLean of the University of California, Davis. It begins by noting that everyone gets tired after concentrating. It is impossible to go a full day with complete concentration on every single task you perform. Your brain simply cannot do it, and it's not a good idea to try.

Maclean's experiment had a group of participants, some who were being trained to meditate and some who weren't, and asked them to watch a series of lines flash on a computer screen and click a mouse when they saw a line that was shorter than the others. It wasn't a very stimulating activity, but that was exactly the point. If they wanted to identify the little changes, then they had to concentrate very intently and for a long time.

Those who were being trained to meditate were significantly more likely to see increasingly small differences between the lines than those who were not meditating. The more meditation training they received, their more their abilities improved. As the paper puts it, their powers of "visual discrimination" had appreciably increased.

This study suggests that meditation can help you concentrate; that was clear. After all, if you are accustomed to sitting silently with your eyes closed, you might be at an advantage for these types of activities. However, the study also found that while meditators were more accurate, they weren't any faster. So the meditators could notice and pick up on these subtle changes between the lines more often than the others, but their speed and reaction times did not differ from the non-meditating participants when they both saw the same line discrepancies on the screen.

This is an important point. It suggests that meditation helps your brain do something automatic—process visual stimuli—but doesn't help with something more complicated, such as improving reaction time.

Nevertheless, meditating is a proven way to help you concentrate on tasks for a longer period of time and remain accurate even if the task is beyond tedious. It can also assist when calm thought and decision-making is a factor. Frustration can often occur as a result of a boring activity, but meditation can help you calm yourself and continue knowing that something needs to be done and it will end soon enough. Patience and a calm attitude can be a good way to improve your concentration and attentiveness while working. At the very least, you'll be used to the semi-boring activity of sitting still and increase your stamina for a dearth of entertainment.

If you're interested in learning to meditate, try practicing breathing exercises when you have a quiet moment of time.

Focus only on your breathing, in and out, and when you're concentrated completely on your breath, then begin to slowly shift your awareness to other parts of your body. For example, move your focus to your heartbeat and then repeat the exercise so that you are focused on nothing else. Then move on again to whatever you like—an arm, an elbow, or even a toe. The purpose is to train yourself and your thoughts to only go in a direction that you want them to go, without getting distracted by stray thoughts so that you can achieve the utmost focus on your task.

Meditation at its core is gaining self-awareness and learning how to channel focus on whatever you choose.

It is not a quick process, and it can often take a long while to learn how to properly center your thoughts so that you can lead them in a specific direction at will. But it is also very beneficial. Meditation can also help in other aspects of your life when calm thoughts and headspace are important, such as making big decisions or investments. Only a few minutes of deep breathing and focused thinking every day may just be the way to improve your concentration and your focus.

Doodling

The last scientifically proven tip to improve focus is doodling. Yes, doodling—the small scribbles or masterpieces that you create in your notebooks or the tiny stick figures you draw in the margins. Apparently doodling isn't as undesirable as we were once told in school.

A psychologist from the University of Plymouth, Jackie Andrade, performed a study to test whether doodling really did have an effect on memory and focus. The participants all listened to a monotonous recording and half of them were asked to doodle while the other half were not. When asked to recall the information they'd just listened to, the doodlers demonstrated significantly higher recall that the non-doodlers.

So why is this the case? It may seem that doodling would only serve as a distraction as it might draw your attention onto whatever you're drawing rather than the task you should be focusing on. However, Andrade argues against this. "People may doodle as a strategy to help themselves concentrate . . . We might not be aware that we're doing it, but it could be a trick that people develop because it helps them from wandering off into a daydream."

This suggests that instead of distracting you and pulling you away from the task, doodling might just be grounding your thoughts and forcing it into a subconscious activity that requires minimal concentration while the rest of you absorbs information.

The scientists hypothesized that unlike daydreaming, which involves a significantly larger mental demand, the mental load required to absentmindedly doodle is quite small and doesn't lead your mind entirely astray from the task that you are supposed to be engaged in. The small iota of your attention that is preoccupied with doodling actually appears to keep you focused and centered in the present time, giving you a release valve from the frustrations of an overly long or tiresome task.

This might also be due to the fact that we are very visual people; our entire world is centered on what you can see. By doing a task such as doodling while you're being bombarded with information, it can help you form associations and therefore you will be able to process things much better.

American author Sunni Brown is known for advertising the power of doodling. According to her research, doodling can help you "anchor a task." This means that it will keep you focused during a long meeting or phone call. Focus on scribbling pictures or designs that reflect what you're hearing or thinking. It doesn't matter if they are funny or weird or have nothing to do with what you are discussing. Doodling will help keep your thoughts from straying and you might be surprised at how much you will be able to recall of a conversation afterward.

If doodling won't work for you, then maybe use the general idea of visual stimuli to help you. When you need to brainstorm ideas, try a pen and paper diagram with as many visual representations as you can. When you have a lot to do, write a physical to-do list and place it somewhere easily accessible so that you will always have it in sight. Or even leave a notebook and pen beside you so that when you hit a stopping point in your work, you can try to reason it out visually. The point is that it may help you organize and focus your thoughts so that you can reach ideas or methods of action.

These were just a few scientifically proven ways to help enhance and maintain your attention. Some may work for you while others don't, or maybe even a combination is what will work the best. The main thing is to take the knowledge from each of these tips and try to apply them in life so that you can better focus on your work. Chew gum when you hit a mental block at work, or try the other oxygen-increasing activities mentioned. Find somewhere quiet to work, practice your meditation, or even doodle in your meetings to try and stay focused. The hardest part is committing to a task and focusing to get it done.

Chapter 10. Conditioning

Being able to focus and quickly on your feet isn't solely reduced to what your brain is capable of. It's also highly related to the condition your brain is in. In other words, let's imagine how an athlete prepares for a big race.

Monica is a runner and it's the night before the national championship. She's going to do her best to not be stressed, and she is going to make sure she gets as much rest as possible. She wants to sleep early and rise late, if possible. She will eat a special meal to ensure she gets the nutrients she needs, and she will drink water every hour, on the hour, to become perfectly hydrated. She meditates for about an hour before sleeping because it clears her mind and pushes the worries and anxieties out of her mind. She needs to prime the engine of her body for optimal performance.

It's almost exactly the same with our brains and mental capacity. They may not be exactly the same factors as how an athlete prepares for a race, but there are far more commonalities than you might expect.

Priming the engine refers to the fact that your brain is your engine, and there are ways of making it run at optimal levels. Ensure that you can think better by taking care of your mental and physical well-being in a few specific ways.

<u>Do Nothing</u>

Burn-out is a very real risk, especially in today's modern age where to get ahead, it seems that everyone has a full-time job as well as a side career that is aimed toward making money. We seek to intentionally pack our days full of activities, professional and social, as a means of squeezing the last drop of enjoyment out of our lives.

Ironically, this quickly becomes counterproductive because very few people have a battery that can function like that. As for what that means for your brain, any shred of fatigue will affect your clarity of thought. That part should be clear from our own lives. We function better on eight hours of sleep versus three hours of sleep.

However, what's less obvious is that disconnecting from everything and doing nothing at all can actually be a path to greater creativity and insight. There's a reason that when we are zoning out at the gym or in the shower, we seem to have a disproportionate amount of epiphanies.Thought is inherently fatiguing and taxing on the mind, and is characterized by the brain emitting beta waves. Relaxation and a lack of attention, on the other hand, is characterized by the brain emitting alpha waves.

What are alpha waves also associated with? Studies by Professor Flavio Frohlich, among others, have shown that alpha waves are associated with enhanced memory, creative thinking, and overall increased happiness.

Maybe that's the reason meditation and practicing mindfulness is being pushed so hard these days. They intentionally slow you down and put you into a state of releasing alpha waves, which triggers increased happiness and life satisfaction. Most of the world's top performers, such as CEOs, always mention meditation as a vital part of their daily routine—this is likely why. The ability to tune things out allows them to function at their peak when it matters, like a battery recharge in the middle of the day.

For the high achievers out there, it's not necessarily a matter of taking a break just to generate some alpha waves. Don't think of it as rest, think of it as recovering so you can get ready when you need to really think creatively.

We instinctively know to sleep, stretch, and warm up our bodies if we have an athletic competition, but we disregard doing the same for our minds. When you relax more and do nothing at all, you enter a state of allowing your mind to wander, and you also come back recharged and refreshed.

Allow yourself to daydream because when was the last time your daydreams were boring and routine versus creative and outlandish? If you need a break, resist the urge to pick up your phone and scroll through your social media. Just staring into blank space might be a better use of your time!

Feed Your Body Right

What your mother told you actually has roots in truth. There are foods that you could classify as good for your brain, but they might not be peas, carrots, and vegetables. Feeding your body so it performs to its peak abilities is about giving your brain the nutrients it wants and needs.

Omega-3 fatty acids aren't produced in the body, which means you must consume them. They've been shown to help brain functioning and are biologically beneficial to the neurons that make up our brain cells. Sixty percent of the human brain is fat (Chang CY, 2009), so omega-3 fatty acids can be said to contribute heavily to the structural integrity of the brain. Glucose, what most food is converted to inside the body, is also the brain's primary source of power.

Finally, omega-3 fatty acids contain EPA and DHA, which act as anti-inflammatories in the brain and body. The main sources of this healthy type of fat are either through supplements, or oily fish such as salmon, sardines, or trout.

Perhaps more fundamental and important than omega-3 fatty acids are simply staying as hydrated as possible. If you aren't hydrated, studies have shown reaction times to decrease by up to 14% (University of East London, 2013). When you're thirsty, your brain is literally busy with the thought of water and how to stave off starvation. In other words, a dehydrated brain is using up to 14% of its resources dealing with feeling thirsty, and you can free up those valuable resources simply by staying hydrated.

Water provides the brain electrical energy for all of its functions, such as thought and memory formation. Brain cells require twice as much energy as other cells in the body, so it makes sense that dehydration would affect your thinking efficacy. After all, your brain can't store it, so it needs a constant supply ready for use, and ready to fuel your focus and clarity of thought.

Studies have shown that if you are only 1% dehydrated, you are likely to have up to a 5% decrease in cognitive function. That rate of decrease compounds the more you get dehydrated. If your memory starts getting fuzzy and you have trouble focusing at 2% dehydration, imagine the complications you'll have at 5-10% dehydration. Further studies have shown that prolonged dehydration causes brain cells to shrink in size and mass. This is most common in the elderly, many of whom tend to be chronically dehydrated for years. Water is also essential for delivering nutrients to the brain and for removing toxins. When the brain is fully hydrated, the exchange of nutrients and toxins will be more efficient—thus ensuring better concentration and mental alertness.

In short, make a habit of carrying a water bottle around with you. You don't need to drink sixty four ounces of water daily as some people might suggest, but you could almost certainly stand to benefit from drinking more than you currently do.

The final overarching tip in eating healthy is to eat to reduce inflammation in your brain. I mentioned this earlier, but inflammation in your brain occurs when special brain cells called microglia are activated (Elmore, 2014). Inflammation in the brain causes neurons to fire more slowly, slowing down mental acuity, recall, and reflexes. Sluggish neurons also shut down the production of energy in the cells. This means that cells fatigue easily, and you may lose your ability to focus for long periods of time.

Unfortunately, there are a whole host of things that tend to activate the microglia and, one of the primary ones being sugar, diary, and gluten. However, there are foods that are naturally anti-inflammatory, such as ginger, green vegetables, and turmeric.

De-stress

Finally, keeping your levels of stress and anxiety low aren't just going to make you a happier person in general, they are going to keep you thinking clearly. It is tackled from a slightly different angle in this chapter.

The body releases a hormone called cortisol as a reaction to stress, anxiety, and fear. Cortisol will raise your blood pressure and keep you tense, because your body senses that there is a threat that might cause you bodily harm.

However, cortisol has also been shown to kill brain cells and cause premature brain aging (Daniela Kaufer, 2014). You also produce fewer brain cells, so stress has the ability to literally shrink your brain. Your existing brain cells for learning and memory function much worse under stress and anxiety.

Finally, chronic stress reduces levels of two critical neurotransmitters: serotonin and dopamine. You might recognize these because they are typically what recreational drugs target because they are tied to pleasure and ecstasy. What happens when you run low on these neurotransmitters? Your brain starts to resemble that of someone with depression (Tafet, 2001).

Manage your stress; manage your brainpower. Diet, exercise, adequate sleep, hydration, and meditation have all been tied to lower stress. Ultimately, stress has power over us because it makes us lose perspective on our lives. It makes us forget the positives we have in our lives, and focus on the small negatives. It's the classic case of not being able to see the forest through the trees. Most of the time, if we stop for a moment and think logically about our stressors, we might find that will be forgotten within the day, and as such, essentially of our own creation.

Slumber

I wanted to end this chapter on another seemingly obvious precursor to better thinking, though it's so obvious it causes everyone to overlook it.

Adequate sleep is one of the most important building blocks of massive focus. Just as we can harken back to the example of the athlete preparing for a race, sleep is that important for optimal brain functioning. Sleep deprivation will affect everything from cognition, to memory, to speed of thought (Killgore, 2010).

Another researcher, Michael Thorpy, commented that "Sleep deprivation will definitely affect one's ability to multitask. Driving is the most intensive multitasking activity we do—it uses hands, feet, vision, awareness of what's going on. When you're sleep-deprived, it strongly affects your ability to multitask. That's why we have so many accidents with cars, and of course trains. Sleep deprivation drains your executive function."

Sleep deprivation has also been shown to have a negative impact on cognitive functions like attention and working memory. Another similar study found that just two hours of sleep deprivation per night resulted in research subjects performing substantially worse on memory and attention-related tasks.

Sleep specifically has wide-ranging effects on memory, which were first reported all the back in 1924. It's not a new discovery. Other studies have shown that getting a full eight hours of sleep after learning a new task can boost recall the next day. Even a one-hour nap has been shown to improve performance in memory-related tasks.

Activity in the hippocampus increases when people enter deep sleep, and this activity is believed to be the brain's method of transferring memory from temporary "working memory" to long-term storage in the neocortex.

Overall, your mother probably scores pretty well with what she nagged you to do when you were younger. Eat *brain* foods, sleep early, and relax to de-stress and do nothing occasionally. All of these are highly important components of setting yourself up for mental success. Remember, a 1% drop in hydration can result in a 5% drop in cognitive abilities. Every little bit counts, especially if you're trying to make a creative breakthrough.

Chapter 11. Nature

The power of nature is a strange one. It has the ability to affect our health and well-being without us even noticing it and can be especially helpful in stressful atmospheres such as at work. There have been many studies showing the positive impact of the environment to not only our moods and attitudes but that being surrounded by nature can have the ability to affect our work patterns and habits and allow us to be more productive in our work.

This doesn't mean that if you work in an office or have a similar job that you need to resign immediately and move to a forest. It doesn't matter where you are but what you can do to take advantage of the world around you. Research has proven that there are several quick and easy things that you can change in your daily work environment so that you are closer to nature and thus taking advantage of all the benefits the natural world can provide us.

The Power of Green

Nature can be calming, soothing, inspiring, and grounding, and it turns out that it's also good when you're having trouble focusing on your work. More specifically, staring at an image associated with nature has been found to be a good way to help improve your working mindset. The *Journal of Environmental Psychology* published a study by University of Melbourne's Kate Lee and a group of colleagues about the power of looking at green.

The experiment was set out with 150 students asked to press a number on their keyboards that corresponded with the series of numbers that flashed repeatedly on a computer screen, unless the number was three, in which case they were to press nothing at all. The activity was long and tedious and required complete concentration and a high attention to detail for a long time.

At the midway point, half the students took a brief 40-second "microbreak" and looked at a specific image on their screens. The study found that by interrupting a tedious, attention-demanding task by looking at a computerized image of a green roof, a roof partially made of vegetation, dramatically improved focus and resulted in better overall performance on their task.

After the students were faced with the image of the green roof, they reported that it felt more "restorative" and that they felt as if they performed better on their task. They performed especially well in their response times, lessening their fluctuation in reactions, and made fewer errors of "omission," in this case failing to tap the keyboard key when they saw a number other than three.

Is it because something in us subconsciously recognizes the primal nature of nature? This could just be because sometimes you just need a break from long monotonous activities in order to reinvigorate yourself. However, it could also be due to the calming effect of nature and its tendency to reduce stress. This is especially true at jobs where you're at a computer all day or reading through paperwork, tasks that can have you feeling physically drained and mentally exhausted.

By breaking up a task that is monotonous and fatiguing and forcing yourself to stare at something that is connected to the natural world, you can actually significantly improve your workflow. A picture or computer background would suffice. Even better, set an alarm and go for a quick walk outside and see nature up close if you can. This is one of the easiest things to achieve in a busy working environment. Hanging a painting, sticking up a poster, or even just searching the Internet will do the trick. A quick 40-second look and you'll be ready to return to any task.

Work In Natural Light

Harsh lighting and artificial light are everywhere. Long gone are the days where we woke with the sun and slept when it set. In today's modern world, we're always trying to fit in as much work as we can and we're not always in the best atmosphere to do so. There are several studies that prove working in natural light is extremely beneficial when trying to complete a task and that too much artificial light can be detrimental in more ways than one.

The Neuroscience Program at Northwestern University conducted one such study. It proved that there is a very strong relationship between workplace daylight exposure and office workers' sleep, activity, and quality of life.

According to the study, employees slept 46 minutes more per night, on average, if they worked in natural light. They also slept more soundly and efficiently and reported a higher quality of life than those who did not work in natural light. Workers who worked in windowless environments had lower scores in their physical health and vitality than those who worked near daylight. They also reported poorer sleep quality, with sleep disturbances and daytime dysfunction.

Natural light has many health-related benefits and can feel mentally more satisfying as well. A lack of natural light has been documented to disrupt the body's circadian rhythms, which are behavioral changes that respond to light and darkness in one's environment. By disrupting our circadian rhythms, a lack of natural light can cause abnormal sleep patterns and also seasonal affective disorder, which results in multiple symptoms such as depression and lethargy.

All of this means that without natural light, your body will be significantly less productive and energized. If you can, try to change your work environment so that you are exposed to natural light as much as possible. If this is impossible, like if you work in an office that is windowless, you can buy natural light lamps that simulate natural light.

A study in Britain, published in *The Responsible Workplace*, also supported the importance of natural light. The study showed that of the many factors that influenced the occupants' level of satisfaction with a building, windows were the number one determinant. This is because the value of lighting is significant in two ways. The first is directly, by affecting our vision—what and how well we are able to see. The second is indirectly, by influencing our moods, behavior, and even hormonal balance.

We've all noticed that when the weather is overcast or it's been raining for days, there can be a dreary atmosphere that sticks around until a ray of light breaks through the clouds. This is because of the strong effect of natural light. Natural light renovations have been shown to result in happy workers and a better overall work environment with less absenteeism and fewer illnesses. Furthermore, because of the satisfaction in the workers from the better lighting, the employees also increased their productivity.

In a final study, Christopher Jung of the University of Colorado showed that bright lights can reduce our level of cortisol, which means that we will feel less stressed under bright lighting conditions.

With all of these benefits of natural light, it seems foolish to prevent ourselves from being exposed to it as often as we can. So stop working like a hermit and open your windows to the sun. If you can't do this, find a way to be exposed to natural light, with a lamp that simulates it if you really have to. Take a walk on your lunch break, sit by a window when you can, or take your work elsewhere. Find a way to bask in the sun's rays and you'll feel all the more better for it. Just wear sunscreen from time to time.

Plants

The more you learn about plants, the more you realize that they will always have additional benefits. If you are someone who works in a room with plants or vegetation of some sort, even if it's just because you think they're pretty or you needed a simple way to decorate, you're already one step ahead of the game. A workplace surrounded by plants is one where you will be considerably more productive and efficient in your tasks.

Several studies have proven the benefits of working with plants around you, even if it's just that small shrub in the corner. One of these studies demonstrated that employees that were randomly assigned to work in a room filled with plants outperformed those who didn't have access to plants.

Another study, conducted in the UK and the Netherlands by Marlon Nieuwenhuis from Cardiff University's School of Psychology, addressed employee perception of plants. When office workers could see a plant from their desks, their perceptions of air quality, concentration, and workplace satisfaction and their objective measures of productivity all increased.

So why are plants so beneficial to have in a workspace? We are all aware of the oxygen-providing attribute of plants, but they are also able to suck carbon dioxide and other relatively benign toxins from the air. This is why the workers perceived to have cleaner and more concentrated air in their offices. But as well as this, plants also appear to provide an overall mental improvement to those in the study. Plants have a considerable calming effect when they surround you, and they've been known to reduce levels of stress. This is perfect for stressful environments like your work. As well as this, plants can help absorb noise, and quiet is often essential for a working environment.

It's not entirely clear just why plants can have such a positive impact on us mentally. Perhaps it's just subconscious or a way to take us out of a stressful work environment by reminding us what's outside or waiting for us when we are finished. Perhaps it's the placebo effect taking hold by the supposed fresher air we are sucking in. Regardless, the evidence is undeniable.

Having a few plants in the office is a quick and easy way to improve your performance and motivation in the office as well as visually liven a place up. The benefits of having even a single plant in your workspace are huge. Not only can you make a place more aesthetically pleasing, you can also improve mood, productivity, and overall performance. Just make sure you take care of it, or choose a hardy one if you're not a green thumb, and your plant will do the rest.

Baby Animals

At last, after all those hours spent staring at adorable newborn pandas or sleeping kittens, the research is finally here to back you up. Maybe that urge to look at cute pictures of baby animals isn't as unproductive as you once thought. You can finally let go of the guilt you've been harboring for "wasting time." Research may be able to prove that looking at cute pictures of baby animals can actually help your productivity at work and improve your overall performance and efficiency.

A Japanese research paper has recently been published in the online journal *PloS One* titled "The Power of Kawaii: Viewing Cute Images Promotes a Careful Behavior and Narrows Attentional Focus." It concluded that looking at cute animal images at work could boost your focus, attention to detail, and overall performance on a task.

The study, conducted by Hiroshi Nottono of the University of Hiroshima, studied three different groups of students as they performed several tasks. These tasks ranged from visual tasks to those involving dexterity, with one of the tasks being similar to the American board game Operation. Each group attempted its respective task twice—the first time without looking at any images and the second time after looking at a series of pictures. These images could have included baby animals, adult animals, or neutral subjects such as foods.

They concluded that the students who viewed cute animal pictures performed far better at their tasks than their peers who viewed pictures of adult animals or food. There are many theorized explanations linked to this improvement.

One reason that was theorized was due to a behavioral tendency in humans to slow down their speech when talking to babies, puppies, and kittens. Researchers speculated that looking at images of baby animals might have had a similar effect in a slowing down of not just speech but the behavior of the students. As such, they were more careful and attentive during their tasks and performed more accurately than their peers.

Another offered explanation was to do with nurturing instincts that may have been brought up when looking at the young animals. The researchers suspected that perhaps those who received an increase in nurturing feelings due to the baby animal pictures might have performed better in care-related tasks that aimed to help someone, even if it was only in the form of a board game.

Whatever the reason, the study determined that the simple act of looking at the photos was enough to increase focus and attention when they were viewed before a task. It stated that "If viewing cute things makes the viewer more attentive, the performance of a non-motor perceptual task would also be improved."

So if you've been secretly viewing these cute pictures at your desk in the office, trying to hide the fact that you may be doing something unproductive, next time just go ahead. Chances are you could be boosting your productivity without you even knowing it.

Generally, the world around us can be far more helpful to our focus and productivity. Nature is all around us and is one thing that is so easily accessible that it would be a complete waste not to take advantage of everything it can give us. Whether it is surrounding ourselves by greenery, natural light, plants, or cute animals, there is always something the world can give us that may help our concentration and our overall motivation. Nature is another way that our literal environments fuel our focus.

Conclusion

At this point a few years after my college experiences as a perpetually-late miscreant, I've gained a new reputation - a stickler for schedules and punctuality.

Of course, I'm the same person who will hike until I get lost, or play video games until the wee hours of the morning. None of that changed, and I don't necessarily restrict myself from my guilty pleasures, except for ice cream on occasion.

I accomplish exactly what I need to, without sacrificing, because of my ability to channel massive focus. Focus is what makes the wheels of the world turn, and it's what will help you create the life you want. I've mentioned it before, and I'll mention it again: focus is the most important of skills because it is the ability to *do*. Without it, you'll be left settling for the silver medal; the second-best; that which comes easy but is not necessarily what you want.

The science is clear, and it provides a blueprint for what to do. Ignore people's anecdotes and fancy systems, and focus on what works for focus. In a sense, make a "don't do" list for focus! What remains will give you crystal clarity structure on your days, tasks, and work. If not, read the book again and design your life for focus.

Best,
Pete
www.petehollins.com

Summary Guide

Chapter 1. Discipline and Willpower

Discipline and willpower are not necessarily the key to focus, but they are needed from time to time. Delayed gratification allows you to postpone what you want to do for what you must do in the moment and can be improved with simple awareness and meta-thinking.

Chapter 2. Goals

Goals are a cornerstone of focus and begin with making sure your environment will enable goals instead of distract from them. Make your default decisions those that affect the outcome you want and get into the habit of using elements of SMART goals. You may not use every one, but you'll see the value of implementing at least one or two at a time.

Chapter 3. Procrastination

Procrastination is the result of the amygdala and the brain's pleasure systems (including dopamine) wanting to carry on instead of suspend enjoyment. After all, we prefer pleasure to pain, and it takes a conscious effort to do the opposite and go against our natural inclination.

Chapter 4. Energy

Managing energy is important because it is a limited quantity. Don't plan to grind for more than 90 minutes without a significant break and understand how your particular circadian rhythm determines when you should push yourself to focus harder.

Chapter 5. Stress

Stress is mostly bad, but a complete lack of stress with regards to focus will essentially mean that you will never care enough to focus intensely. Therefore, you are at your best when you are in the sweet spot in terms of the Yerkes-Dodson Curve.

Chapter 6. Singletasking

Multitasking is a myth. We do this more often than we realize through simply switching tasks frequently. Replace this with singletasking and focusing on a single task for an extended period of time, such as Cal Newport recommends.

Chapter 7. Odds and Ends

The odds and ends of focus come in both counterintuitive and intuitive forms: chewing gym, meditation, doodling, and seeking solitude.

Chapter 8. Nature

The power of nature, whether placebo or real, pays dividends for your focus. Look at more green, look at more animals, go outside more, and keep plants around for maximum productivity.

Chapter 9. Productivity

Productivity starts with tracking everything so there is a visible sense of progress for encouragement and record-keeping, using implementations, and creating motion and momentum before noon.

Chapter 10. Tactics

There are a few specific tactics you can employ on a daily basis for improved focus, such as using the ABCDE priority list, implementing batching, avoiding negative media, and creating a don't-do list.

Chapter 11. Conditioning

Just like the body, the brain has optimal conditions in which it can focus. These elements come together in the form of sleep, rest, and nutrition—nothing surprising. If the brain is not conditioned and rested, then you might as well give up for the day.

www.ingramcontent.com/pod-product-compliance
Lightning Source LLC
Chambersburg PA
CBHW071159070526
44584CB00019B/2853